From Porric   Fie..

A SCOTTISH FAMILY LIVING IN HONG KONG

Howard Gee

Biography

Howard Gee was born and educated in Edinburgh and has worked, travelled and lived throughout Europe and the Far East with his family. Howard is married to Carmine and they have two grown up children and four Grandchildren who are now all very happy to be living in the shadows of the Wallace Monument near Stirling and the magnificent Ochil Hills.

Whilst serving in the Scots Guards, Howard was selected into the Army Physical Training Corps and was involved on active service with the Brigade of Gurkhas in Borneo and with other regiments throughout troubled areas of the world. He served in all Non Commissioned Ranks including Regimental Sergeant Major and was commissioned into the APTC in 1980. He is now retired and writing his memoires; the first of which is titled 'We Were Only Bairns'. The follow-up book 'Boots and Bearskins' is a riotously funny story of army life. Both books let the reader glimpse another world as truth mingles with humour.

Works by Howard Gee

We Were Only Bairns
Growing Up In Edinburgh In The
Forties And Fifties

(Book 1 from the 'There and Back' series)

Boots and Bearskins
Life As A Recruit In The Scots Guards

(Book 2 from the 'There and Back' series)

From Porridge To Paddy Fields
A Scottish Family Living In Hong
Kong

(Book 3 from the 'There and Back' series)

To my family who have encouraged me to keep writing.

Contents

Preface...1

Chapter 1 - Arrival at Kai Tak 2

Chapter 2 - Sui Pak Villa 10

Chapter 3 - The Gurkhas.....................................22

Chapter 4 - Hong Kong 28

Chapter 5 - Sek Kong 34

Chapter 6 - Dashera...38

Chapter 7 - Christmas at Sek Kong 45

Chapter 8 - Khud Race...57

Chapter 9 - Around Hong Kong............................63

Chapter 10 - Borneo 77

Chapter 11 - Stand To 84

Chapter 12 - A Tragedy 91

Chapter 13 - The Kelabit People..........................98

Chapter 14 - Dragon Boat Festival.....................108

Chapter 15 - The Cross Harbour Race..............114

Chapter 16 - Start of another Year 120

Chapter 17 - The Nepal Cup...............................124

Chapter 18 - A Super Star 129

Chapter 19 - Sunshine on the Water..................135

Chapter 20 - Fanling Furniture 141

Chapter 21 - Tokyo 145

Chapter 22 - Judo Training..................................154

Chapter 23 - Black Belt Grading.........................160

Chapter 24 - Farewell to Hong Kong..................169

Preface

After transferring from the Scots Guards to the Army Physical Training Corps, Howard was posted in 1965 to the Headquarters, 48 Gurkha Infantry Brigade, Hong Kong accompanied by his wife Carmine and their young son Andrew.

When 1st 6th Queen Elizabeth's Own Gurkha Rifles went to Borneo on active service during the Indonesian Confrontation, Howard as a young sergeant went with them.

The adventures that he experienced throughout Hong Kong, Brunei, Borneo, Singapore, Malaya, Japan and other corners of the Far East are about a way of life that very few have been fortunate to experience and are told with sincerity and humour alike.

Chapter 1 - Arrival at Kai Tak

It was a sunny afternoon in July 1965 when we left Scotland for Hong Kong. My new army posting was to Headquarters 48 Gurkha Infantry Brigade and I was accompanied by Carmine and our young son Andrew of 2 years and 10 months. It had been a long journey of 38 hours as flights were not being allowed over Vietnam airspace because of the war situation. As such, we had three refuelling stops with short breaks in the terminals at Istanbul, Bombay and Bangkok. As I closed my eyes and relaxed I could hear the soothing hum of the plane's engines as it flew onwards to our destination in the Far East

I was dreaming and the word idle kept coming into my mind, a throwback from the days of my service in the Scots Guards from 1959 to1962 before I was selected to transfer into the Army Physical Training Corps. After a three year posting to Troon in Scotland where Andrew was born I, Sergeant Instructor Howard Gee, much to our delight, was posted to serve with Gurkha Regiments in British Forces Post Office1 (Hong Kong).

'Idle' had been a common word used in the Brigade of Guards when drill instructors were shouting abuse at the guardsmen; usually meaning lazy and useless. Idle on parade, idle salute, idle haircut. 'idle little man,' shouted one Lance Sergeant at a six foot four inch guardsman on sentry duty. I remember even a duty piper being bawled at and threatened with being thrown into the guardroom for, according to the duty Lance Corporal, conduct prejudicial to good order and military discipline in that he did play his bagpipes in an insolent and idle manner. One could be a murderer, a train robber, an arsonist and other terrible things but none would be considered as bad in the army world as being 'idle.'

'Howard, waken up,' I heard Carmine say as she nudged me. 'You were smiling in your sleep. The Captain has just announced that we are approaching Hong Kong and all safety belts are to be fastened.'

'Oh I was dreaming,' I said. 'Is Andrew OK?'

'I think so,' said Carmine, 'he's a wee bit pale.' She lifted her head to glance out the window and suddenly gasped. The plane approaching the runway appeared to be plunging into the sea. Suddenly we could see and almost reach out and touch the villagers in their shanty town of huts perched on the rising ground either side of the runway. Arriving in Hong Kong was an experience ingrained on one's mind forever and sighs of relief could be heard throughout the plane as the wheels touched terra firma and it taxied towards its allocated berth. After some minutes when the engines had been switched off, the doors were opened by the cabin crew allowing the smells of Hong Kong and the heat of the afternoon to rush in. The Captain's voice came over the PA system 'Welcome to Hong Kong.'

I lifted down the hand luggage from the rack which we had agreed Carmine could manage to carry off the plane. I slipped on my blazer and picked up Andrew to carry him down the aisle and off the plane. Andrew who was trying to keep awake, closed his eyes, put his head on my shoulder and was suddenly sick down my neck; poor lad, it had been a long, long journey. At least, I thought to myself as I stepped down off the plane and experienced the foul smells in the air of Kowloon, the smell of sickness around me wouldn't be noticed. Welcome to Hong Kong announced a female voice from the terminal PA.

We were met at the airport by SSI Des Burges APTC from HQ 48 Brigade whom I was taking over from. He handed a couple of welcomed sweat rags (small towels) to us. He then drove us to The Golden Gate Hotel in Kowloon where we had been booked into for a few days allowing us to find our feet and start to acclimatise before we moved the 20 miles up into to the New Territories where the Gurkha Regiments were based.

The air conditioning of the hotel was bliss and after a shower and a meal we wandered outside to have a look at Kowloon. The noise of the ivories from the games of mah-jong being slapped down on the tables in conjunction with the locals shouting in high pitched tones, various dialects of Cantonese and Mandarin, created a sound which seemed like a continuous argument that we had never experienced before. It seemed that almost all adults in Hong Kong gambled at mah-jong late into the nights and early mornings. We heard that often disputes were solved with the misuse of meat cleavers. After a short walk, we were ready to return to the hotel, shower again and jump into bed. We slept soundly that night despite the noise coming into our room from the streets. After breakfast the following morning, we ventured once more out on to the hustling, bustling streets of Kowloon.

We wandered up one side of Nathan Road, the main artery of Kowloon where bamboo poles laden with drying clothes hung out of almost every window along with Chinese banners and flags from high buildings where sounds of Chinese music poured from the windows and filled the hot still air. We were mesmerised by the variety of shops and the numerous roadside food stalls where hot sizzling food was being cooked emanating culinary smells that were new to our nostrils. Customers sat on small stools shovelling heaps of rice from bowls into their mouths with chopsticks at all times of the day and night. The small shops and stalls were crammed with sacks of coloured spices and trays of varieties of dried fish and shrivelled creatures which we couldn't even guess at what they were. Livestock was being sold from every kind of basket and container imaginable. It seemed the custom was only to buy creatures that were still living and breathing prior to cooking and eating them, including toads, frogs, snakes and varieties of other creepy crawlies. We crossed the very busy road where a policeman standing on a pedestal was directing traffic ranging from large painted and decorated lorries, cars and taxies to bicycles and rickshaws. Passengers getting on and off buses were carrying trussed up chickens, ducks, varieties of fish in bags full of water and even small piglets. Women carried their babies tucked into shawls strapped to their backs; many men and women wore Chinese style tops and wide flowing trousers.

When we reached the harbour, we stood in awe of the large numbers of Chinese junks ploughing up, down and across the harbour from Kowloon to Hong Kong Island. They carried families who lived, washed, slept and ate aboard them, not to mention hanging over the sides for the toilet even when the waves were high and rough. Ferries, fishing boats, huge American naval warships and aircraft carriers were bringing servicemen into the Colony on Rest and Recuperation from Vietnam. The US sailors and marines filled the bars and nightclubs; keeping their own naval police, as well as the Hong Kong Custom Officers and police patrols on land and sea alert and busy. Looking through this panorama of moving vessels lay Hong Kong Island just over a mile away. It was sad to hear that shortly after we arrived in the Colony that on two separate occasions planes returning servicemen to Vietnam, sped down the Kai Tak runway, failed to take off, went off the end of the runway and ditched into the sea with very few survivors.

From a stall beside the harbour we bought soft drinks and some Chinese mixed cracker biscuits to nibble whilst Andrew tucked into an ice cream. We found a seat and enjoyed the cool breeze drifting off the sea as we watched a way of life roll by. It seemed like living a dream. We had spent the last three years living by the sea at Troon in Scotland but this scene in front of us now was very different.

The air was very humid and as advised we had purchased from a shop bottles of water and some small sweat towels which we carried with us at all times; sweat just poured off us continually and sun tan cream was a must especially for Andrew. We did our best to stay in the shade wearing caps which we bought from one of the many stalls on the kerb. We had been advised before leaving UK that once we moved up to the New Territories, local tailors and tradesmen would call at our doors and would make suits, shirts, shorts, shoes for Master and light dresses for Missy; all handmade to measure at very cheap prices (8 HK dollars to £1); as long as you allowed an unbelievable delivery time of 24 hours. We strolled slowly back to the hotel, had showers and sat on the balcony wrapped in bath towels before changing for our evening meal. Carmine and Andrew were taking it all in their stride but we were still finding it hard to contain our excitement about life ahead.

The following morning I had an early breakfast at 0645hours and was ready and waiting for the Gurkha driver. When he arrived in a land rover he took me to meet my new Company Commander at the Headquarters 48 Gurkha Infantry Brigade at Sek Kong which lay at the heart of the New Territories; 20 miles north towards the Chinese Border.

Carmine intended to spend the day with Andrew browsing shops around Nathan Road and generally acclimatising to the heat and our new lifestyle. One of her first tasks when we moved up to Sek Kong would be to interview for an amah who would carry out house cleaning, washing, ironing and other chores around the house including babysitting as required when social functions were on in the mess. As families were posted home to the UK, amahs were recommended to incoming families. The daily work routine, hours of work, times required, and the wage which was usually standard throughout the families was discussed and agreed upon. Each army quarter had an amah's room if sleeping arrangements were required and the whole system generally worked well with amahs speaking English fairly well, 'missy' learning some Cantonese and with both understanding sign language it wasn't long before communications were almost perfect. The amah's dress for work was generally a very simple floral or coloured sleeveless Mandarin style top with a round neck and buttons down the front; trousers were often in a dark colour. Bare feet were the order of the day around the house and when working outside, a round type of straw hat with a black circular veil to keep out the sun was worn similar to the Hakka women who worked daily in the paddy fields.

To reach Sek Kong by road, there were two ways; one was the long coastal route by the Castle Peak Road and the other a shorter distance of 20 miles over the 'TWISK' which had been built by military engineers some years before. The name derived from TW representing Tsun Wan (area of Kowloon where the road started) adding the IS to become 'TWIS' represented the twisting road up past the summit of Tai Mo Shan, the local mountain between Kowloon and the route to the border of China. SK on the end stood for the end destination SEK KONG thus the route was named the 'TWISK'.

I was met at the Company office by QMSI Alex Spoors, the Senior Warrant Officer APTC who welcomed me and introduced me to the Officer Commanding Headquarter Company, Major Lorimar 7Gurkha Rifles. I then met WO1 Nelson and most of the other members of staff before commencing a familiarisation tour of the area. At the office in the gymnasium, Sergeant Instructor Dave Jordan APTC who was attached to 49 Regiment RA was waiting to greet me.

'A good flight out Howard?' he asked. 'I bet you felt the heat when you got out of the plane. I look forward to meeting Carmine and young Andrew. It will take time for them to adjust but I know that they will enjoy the lifestyle here.'

'Thanks,' I said, 'it was a long journey and we were glad to land safely on the runway and not in the sea. We are looking forward to life out here. I've never seen so many people making so much noise; bicycles everywhere and so many stalls selling hot sizzling food of every description.'

'You'll love it,' he said. 'Once you are settled in, Geishla, my wife and I will have you over for Sunday lunch. She's looking forward to having a good old chat with Carmine. It will be a chance to catch up with the news from UK although she herself is from Germany and she can tell Carmine about the way of life out here.'

'Sounds great thank-you, we'll look forward to that.'

QMSI Alex Spoors whose tour of duty in Hong Kong was coming to an end was shortly to be replaced by QMSI Ivan Goodwin arriving from the Army School of Physical Training Aldershot. 'In the next few days Howard, I'll take you round the various barracks to meet the Commanding Officers of the Gurkha Regiments and their senior officers,' he said. 'They are all very keen to meet you and discuss the objectives of their fitness programmes. You will be responsible for the timescales of achievement in conjunction with the introduction of programmes for the teaching of swimming which is a weakness of Gurkha soldiers hailing from the mountainous regions of Nepal. With the possibility in the near future of active service in Borneo involving the regiments, soldiers will be required to traverse fast flowing rivers in full combat kit carrying necessary weapons and equipment. They must have the confidence in their ability to do it and be fit to fight when they reach their targets. Each regiment already has within their companies, trained Assistant Physical Training Instructors who have qualified at the Far East Land Forces School of PT in Singapore and they will make up your training staff. It will be a great help if you can learn to speak Gurkhali which all Gurkhas speak and understand; it's a derivation of the many Nepalese dialects.'

'I'll do my best,' I thought to myself. I had been told that in some ways, Gurkhali was guttural and sounded a bit like Scots. Perhaps it was the mountainous air and the stirring of the bagpipes which we had in common; each regiment had its own pipe band as well as a military band which were very popular when performing around the world including at the Edinburgh Tattoo.

I met the Families Officer based in his office in Sek Kong village which was approximately two miles from the camp. He explained that at present there were no available quarters in the village but he had arranged for us to move into a flat within Sui Pak Villa at Fanling near the Chinese Border until a quarter became available. He assured me that as a family we would be very happy there and would have the company of other families from the HQ staff. He arranged for me to be driven up to view the Villa by one of his staff over the lunch period and as we drove through the large iron gates of Sui Pak Villa, I knew that we were going to enjoy living there.

Back at the hotel that evening, I had so much to tell Carmine especially about Sui Pak Villa; its swimming pool, magnificent gardens and floral abundance with varieties of birds and strutting peacocks. I told her how the fountains and an ornamental Chinese bridge

8

stretching over a pond full of multi coloured tropical fish swimming amongst the large green pads of water lilies enhanced the ambience of the surroundings. The house was owned and lived in by Mr. Chow a Chinese millionaire and his family. As for travelling, I would be able to share a lift to and from the camp approximately 12 miles distant until I could arrange to purchase a car. The programme was that the following day I would continue my familiarisation tour of the camp and the day after we would travel as a family to our new home at Sui Pak Villa.

It was so hot but we had been given all the correct inoculations before leaving UK and been briefed on the necessary precautions such as taking daily paludrin tablets and sleeping under mosquito nets. We had been warned not to drink water from the tap but to boil or buy bottles of already boiled water which were sold very cheaply and literally on every street corner; stay in the shade where possible, wear light clothing with suitable headgear and ensure that sun tan lotion applied daily was of the correct strength keeping prickly heat at bay.

It was a whole new life for our family and we were very excited. Our three year tour of duty in Hong Kong had begun.

Chapter 2 - Sui Pak Villa

It was a warm humid morning as we drove to Sui Pak Villa which was like an oasis amongst the miles of flat paddy fields which was an encouragement to any driver to concentrate on the road or possibly end up with the rice plants in a paddy field.

When we arrived as a family at Sui Pak Villa for the first time, we were welcomed by Su Hadkis and Jean Murray who were to be our immediate neighbours. Our MFO boxes containing our personal belongings and clothes had left Troon some months before us to travel by sea and now, courtesy of the Quartermaster's Department, had arrived in the Colony and been delivered to our new albeit temporary home.

'How are you?' asked Su. 'I heard it was a long journey especially for Andrew,' she said giving him a cuddle.

'We are getting over it and looking forward to settling in to life here in Hong Kong,' replied Carmine

'Nice to meet you,' said Jean, shaking Carmine's hand in a warm welcoming fashion. 'I'm sure that you will enjoy living at Sui Pak Villa even if it is just until a quarter is available in the village. Anything that we can do to help you settle in, just shout.'

'Thank-you very much,' Carmine and I said in unison.

'Mr Chow wishes to invite you this evening for a traditional Chinese meal and rice wine to welcome you to his home,' said Su. 'In fact we are all invited. You will be able to meet Arthur my husband and Tommy our son who is presently at the primary school in the village and Jean's husband Dave. No need to dress up,' she quickly added with a smile.

'That's great,' said Carmine, 'and Andrew will have a friend to play with.'

'I'll show you to your flat,' said Su. 'If you want to unpack, I'll prepare some lunch and we can have it on the balcony in my flat next door to you. We are going to be neighbours.'

Thank-you very much,' answered Carmine, giving Andrew a wee cuddle as she pointed towards the swimming pool. 'You are going to like it here Andrew,' she said.

Thank goodness I have been given the day off and it's Friday, I thought to myself; start of the week-end. 'I'll get the luggage up to the flat and we can start unpacking.' I shouted.

'Let me know when you are ready for lunch,' said Su. 'Perhaps you would like a cold drink now?'

'I think Andrew might be ready for one,' said Carmine.

'A glass of orange juice coming up, especially for you Andrew,' said Su with a smile. She had a natural way with children

The flat was small but clean and comfortable looking and would be suitable until a quarter became available in the village. The sitting room was reasonably spacious with a long green curved settee fitting around the wall, a dining table, chairs, glass cabinet, coffee table and other furnishings all neatly laid out. The bedroom had a tiled floor which would be cool on the feet, a double and a single bed, wardrobe, chest of drawers and a couple of bedside tables with carved figure lamps. Blinds on the window would also help to keep the room cool as would the large fan hanging down from the ceiling. The balcony overlooking the garden was a real gem where wind chimers hanging in the trees were playing melodic sounds in the balmy breezes and I immediately thought about us passing the hours away whilst enjoying refreshing drinks and moments of relaxation. The bathroom had a shower, a corner fitting bath and a matching coloured bidet. Unfortunately it was a shared kitchen but Carmine was sure that she would be able to work out and agree the usage with Su. The amahs were used to sharing and worked well together.

That evening, we met Arthur and Dave before meeting Mr. Chow, his wife and family. Mr. Chow was a small man who had short dark hair, a round face carrying a smile, a warm countenance and very alert eyes. He was dressed in traditional Chinese costume and bowed slightly holding out his hands in a welcoming gesture to us. We had been told that Mr. Chow had several wives who shared the cleaning, cooking and general chores of the house. I could appreciate the idea of several wives and the thought crossed my mind that afterwards, I might sound Carmine out. Och, perhaps not.

'You are very welcome to my home,' he said in a quiet voice as he touched Andrew's shoulder.

'Thank-you,' I said. 'It's a pleasure to meet you Mr. Chow. This is my wife Carmine and our son Andrew.'

'Please join me,' he said, turning towards a large table full of prepared countless dishes of varieties of cooked hams and meats, the centre-piece of which was a decorated piglet with an apple in its mouth. Beef and chicken dishes, sea foods, fish, rice fried and boiled, sweet and sour foods and varieties of vegetables. As we sat down at the table we were served with bowls of noodles and bean soup. Fresh fruit, nuts and moon cakes not to mention soft drinks, rice wine, San Miguel and Tiger beers adorned an adjoining table. The younger members of Mr. Chow's family took great delight in teaching us how to use chopsticks and had much laughter at our efforts. It was a lovely meal and a wonderful welcome to Sui Pak Villa.

Su recommended to Carmine, Ah Cum, an amah who had previously worked at the Villa. Arthur told me about a Warrant Officer in 49 Regiment who was returning to UK on promotion and was selling his car, a black and white Simca which I bought the following week. Travelling independently was a must especially when visiting various Gurkha Regiments based throughout the New Territories. As Hong Kong drivers drove on the left as we did back home, I had no worries about the driving but the congested traffic and density of people using the roads not to mention the abundance of luggage and livestock that they carried in conjunction with buses, lorries, yellow taxi cabs, bikes and rickshaws made me realise that I would have to take it steady at first. Everyone told us that we would get used to it if we survived the first few months.

The local villagers were always smiling and waving to us whenever we left the Villa. The children going to school in the morning all wore open neck white shirts or blouses portraying the school badge, dark shorts or skirts, white socks and black shoes and looked very smart. All carried satchels across their shoulders full of school books and packed lunches. As they walked along in groups, they never stopped talking and always seemed to have a smile on their cheery faces.

The shops and the market at Fanling could only be reached either by car or walking across the surrounding paddy fields where the Hakka women in rolled up dark trousers, stood in water up to their knees as they planted or harvested the rice. Watching the huge oxen pulling the wooden ploughs through the channels of water during rice planting was like stepping back in time and looking at scenes of ancient China. The fertilising of the fields with raw oxen dung carried in buckets balanced on poles across their shoulders by barefooted women and men before being tipped into the fields was a system that had been repeated over thousands of years. The smell was putrid but the rice produced was part of their staple diet. I thought that it was probably better not to think too much about the process when eating it.

It was one of those quiet peaceful afternoons when Carmine had gone to the market for some vegetables and Andrew was playing in the garden with Tommy who had a half-day from school. Andrew, who had decided to go and find his mum, slipped out of the gates and wandered off in the direction of the market. Ah Cum suddenly realised that he was missing and had everyone searching the garden whilst she herself made off towards the market. Ah Cum in a terrible state eventually returned with Andrew who was covered from head to foot in paddy field slime and manure and smelling like a steaming dung heap; he was clutching a toy that Ah Cum had bought him from a stall. She had just got home when Carmine returned, quite unaware of the situation.

'I'm so sorry Missy,' said Ah Cum. 'Andrew went to the market to find you. He slipped and fell into the paddy field but was lifted out quickly by one of the workers; Very, very sorry Missy.'

13

'Are you alright Andrew?' asked Carmine.

'Yes Mum, but a bit smelly.' he replied totally unaware of the commotion and worry that had caused.

'You were naughty not returning to Ah Cum when she called you. Right let's get you into a bath and get you scrubbed. Everything is OK Ah Cum, nothing for you to worry about. Go and have a break. Have a cup of your special tea and we'll see you in a while and thank you for rescuing him

'Thank-you Missy.'

Carmine told me that she lifted Andrew into the bath, scrubbed him, lifted him out, dried him and gave him a big hug. Andrew smiled at his mum, enjoying the attention that he was receiving; still oblivious to the whole picture of concern and worry.

We spent the week-end relaxing in the shade of the garden and swimming in the pool. Arthur had popped over to the 'Better Hole' local village pub in Fanling and returned with a carrier of Tiger beer, lemonade and some soft drinks. Su brought nuts and nibbles down from the house and both joined us at the pool as the afternoon sun streamed through the tall palms and trees blossoming with lychees (a favourite Hong Kong fruit).

After listening to our story of arriving from Troon in Scotland and the journey out here, Arthur explained that as he was a Bombardier in the Royal Artillery based at HQ 48 Brigade, he already knew of my pending arrival at the Headquarters.

Su told us her story of being born in a part of China where the local tradition still believed that women should have tiny feet and regardless of the real cruelty involved, she, shortly after being born had her feet bound tightly with bandages. It was only when she had ran away from home and escaped over the border into British controlled Hong Kong that she had been relieved of the terrible pain and the harsh way of life that many children in China suffered. She had met Arthur, married and had Tommy. Although her English wasn't fluent, she had a lovely personality and couldn't do enough to help Carmine settle into life in Hong Kong. Andrew and Tommy played well together and before long were inseparable.

I was looking forward to starting work the following day at the gymnasium in Sek Kong. Su had offered to take Carmine and Andrew by bus to meet some friends in Sek Kong and have lunch at the village pool which would give Carmine an opportunity to see the quarters, shops, NAFFI, school and amenities in the village.

Carmine and I agreed that the following Saturday, we would take Andrew on an exciting journey travelling by train from Fanling to Kowloon and catch the ferry across to Hong Kong Island to see the sights. It was like living in a dream; a combination of the world's busiest place within the warmth of a gigantic greenhouse. It was a magical world with so much still to explore. Andrew was excited and so were we.

Mr Chow's living room
Sui Pak Villa

Bedtime
Sui Pak Villa

Carmine on the bridge at Sui Pak Villa

Sui Pak Villa

Howard and Andrew at Sui Pak Villa

Carmine with amahs

Chapter 3 - The Gurkhas

I decided that the first regiment that I would visit on Monday afternoon was 1/6th Queen Elizabeth's Own Gurkha Rifles based at Gallipoli Barracks in the New Territories and although I was wearing my APTC Vest, white shorts, white socks and PT shoes, the Sergeant of the Guard efficiently inspected my ID Card. I was then greeted by 'Ramro Din (good day) PT Sergeant' as he stood to attention and with a broad grin on his face, waved me through the gates pointing in the direction with his chin of the Second in Command's office.

As I drove passed the square I watched in amazement as a platoon was being drilled in quick time by a Company Sergeant Major. The platoon were carrying rifles and their little stocky legs were going backwards and forwards inside their starched and pressed wide bottomed shorts trying to keep up to the rhythm of a very fast tune being played by a piper from the regimental pipe band. I knew that Gurkha Regiments on parade marched with a very quick step as our own Light Infantry did, reminiscent of days in battle when moving quickly from one position to another was vital. It was fascinating to watch and I realised that they were probably rehearsing to take over the guard duties the following morning. They were immaculately dressed in their wide brimmed hats, pressed short sleeve shirts and shorts carrying an SLR rifle with a bayonet on their left hip and a kukri on the right hip. Their long dark socks and puttees complimented their highly polished gleaming boots; all their kit would be cleaned and pressed again for the inspection to-morrow morning prior to guard mounting.

Before coming out to Hong Kong, I was aware that the Gurkha soldier in general was of the Hindu religion and came from the Himalayan Kingdom of Nepal where Britain has had close ties for over 150 years. After winning a war against Nepal, the British Powers of the day was so impressed by the fighting ability of their enemy that they encouraged them to serve in Her

22

Majesty's Service.

Each year 11000 potential recruits apply for approximately 170 places in the British Army Gurkhas; the two Recruiting Depots in Nepal are Paklihawa in the West and Dharan in the East, and the Training Depot was at Sungei Patani, North Malaysia. Their distinguishing characteristics are Mongolian in appearance, a natural physical strength, short and stocky in stature with strong thighs and calves; they run well uphill and are unbeatable on a downhill slope. They have a happy disposition with qualities of honesty, loyalty and courage and when asked for a direction, tend to use their chin to point the way. They have the ability to work hard, march for long periods of time and then fight as required with tenacity and military strength when they reach their target. The British Gurkhas are mainly recruited from the Nepali hill tribes of Gurungs and Magars from the West and Central Nepal and Rais and Limbus from the East. Their motto is 'Better to die than be a coward'.

All Gurkhas carry the famous kukri which is a sharp, curved knife with a blade over 12 inches long and is prominent on their various regimental cap badges. When brandishing in anger with their war cry of 'Ayo Gurkhali' they do live up to their fearsome reputation. Two smaller tools are held in the top of scabbard; the karda is a sharp skinning knife whilst the chakmak is blunt and used to hone the kukri blade.

Mount Everest, the tallest mountain in the world lies in the heart of Nepal and was climbed for the first time in 1953, the year that Queen Elizabeth had her Coronation.

The 6th Queen Elizabeth's Own Gurkha Rifles and the 7th Duke of Edinburgh's own Gurkha Rifles are recruited from the West of Nepal whilst The 2nd King Edward V11's Own Gurkha Rifles (The Sirmoor Rifles) and The 10th Princess Mary's own Gurkha Rifles are recruited from the East.

The camp buildings were sparkling white in the afternoon sunshine and the whole camp area was spotlessly clean. Soldiers were in orderly groups, marching or running everywhere with the aim of reaching their objectives and carrying out their daily duties, tasks and instructions efficiently and as quickly as possible. Some sections dressed in combat kit were carrying rifles for weapon training; some dressed in PT kit were heading for the playing fields and possibly the assault course whilst some wives carrying babies with laughing, chatting children by their sides were walking from the direction of the school.

The aroma of freshly made curry was wafting over from the cookhouse and I was tempted to call in and give my greetings to the cook Sgt. Major; I made a mental note to visit him next time. I parked the car and headed for the stairs that led up to a balcony which stretched along the front of the Headquarters block distinguishable by the Brigade and Battalion flags flying in the light morning breeze.

I was met at the top of the stairs by Captain Henderson, the Training Officer and I felt quite at home when I heard his Scottish accent. He introduced me to the Commanding Officer and the Second in Command both of whom made me very welcome.

'I hope that you will enjoy working with our soldiers.' said Lieutenant Colonel Hickey. 'Perhaps you will learn to converse with them.'

I assured them both that I was looking forward to starting work and would do my best to learn Gurkhali and respect the traditions and ways of life of the Regiment

'That's good to hear,' said the Colonel. 'I don't think any PT Instructors have achieved learning the language before. Major Richards and the Training Officer Captain Henderson I know wish to discuss the training programme with you to ensure that we are ready to successfully complete the role that we have been tasked to carry out. In December 1962 President Sukarno of Indonesia started a confrontation by claiming land from Malaysia who asked the British Government for support. We flew into Sarawak in February 1964 and again earlier this year (1965) on operational tours. The battalion must be fully fit for active service again in Borneo next year to be based at Bario.'

'You would be invaluable to the battalion in

Borneo; visiting the companies in their locations, ensuring that their morale was kept high when not on patrol through organising circuit training and general fitness with whatever equipment was available in their jungle camps not to mention some sports and recreation such as volleyball. Perhaps you would join us when we are called.'

'That would be great sir,' I said wondering what I'd let myself in for.

'Good to have you with us,' said the Colonel. 'I have a Brigade Conference to attend and will leave you now with Major Richards and Captain Henderson.'

'Thank-you sir,' I said.

'Please sit down staff,' said Major Richards gesturing to myself and Captain Henderson. It was normal for sergeants and staff sergeants in the APTC to be called staff.

'My main concern,' said Major Richards, 'is to ensure that our soldiers are physically and mentally fit to carry their equipment and weapons in the heat of the jungle and be able to successfully use them when they reach their objectives. I am also concerned about the very fast flowing rivers we will have to cross and I don't intend to lose any of the regiment because they are not strong enough swimmers. Can you help us staff with our swimming training?'

'Yes sir, I can and will be glad to.'

'We would also like to arrange a training programme for our Nepal Cup Football Team, cross country team and our selected teams for the Inter Company Khud Race. Of course you will be invited to attend the Battalion Dashera Festival and the evening celebrations to which Mrs. Gee will also be invited. I would very much like you to arrange and train a gymnastic display team in the arena with the school children.

'Thank you sir,' I said, again wondering what I was letting myself in for; Khud Race? Dashera?

After meeting the Gurkha Assistant Instructors and a quick tour of the camp, I said, 'Dhaniyabad aru bida' (thanks and good-bye) to the Senior Gurkha Sergeant Major who walked back to the car with me.

'Staff, please come and have breakfast with us in the mess one morning; any morning. Reveille is 0600hrs when we start the day with a hot mug of tea and stop for breakfast at 0800hrs. You will enjoy the baht; rice, chillies, goats meat and lamb,' (bakra and dumba).

'Wow!!' I thought to myself, 'from porridge to paddy fields; what a contrast!'

'Oh and may I suggest that you purchase a bamboo umbrella to carry around with you as the monsoon season is not too distant and when it rains it starts without warning and fills the monsoon ditches very quickly.

'I will and thanks again, Sergeant Major, see you soon.'

On the way home I called into 29 Mule Pack Company at Lo Wu Camp set back in the hills. The Company had proved to be indispensable during the Second World War when the mules were used to supply rations and ammunition to the British soldiers based deep in the hills near the Chinese border. Their role was to defend Hong Kong against the invading Japanese.

The Company recruited from the local Chinese Hong Kong population and were the only Company left of its kind in the British Army. They were a real cheery lot who made me welcome and said that they would be delighted if I could help and coach them with their sports. Basketball was their favourite and both courts were almost continuously used in their spare time; closely followed by football and volleyball. Most of their work involved carrying supplies on the mules into the hills to troops on training exercises, in case such a scenario as with the Japanese ever again arose. Time was also spent training the mules of which there was over eighty, mucking out the stables and carrying out general military duties as required. I don't think that they had seen a PT Instructor for some time and when I promised them that I would return as soon as I had visited all my other units, I got a big cheer as I left the camp.

It had been a long day but I felt that I had been made welcome everywhere and already I was settling in with a real job of work to do. To-morrow I would meet some of the other units, study their training programmes and would advise on raising their standard of fitness, coaching their team sports and encouraging their leisure and recreational activities as required by the Brigadier of the Headquarters at 48 Brigade.

I felt the satisfaction of having a good day as I drove through the gates of Sui Pak Villa and was conscious of the warm sun touching my shoulders as I stepped out of the car and into the garden; already it felt like coming home after a day's work.

'Had a good day darling?' asked Carmine handing me a much welcomed San Miguel beer which I just managed to put down on an ornamental table as Andrew came running out of the house and jumped into my arms. As I put my arm around Carmine and gave her a cuddle, she smiled and I knew that in spite of having to sleep under Mosquito nets, take paludrine tablets daily and sit under swirling fans after a hot shower watching the chit chats (small harmless lizards) running up and down the walls, we would enjoy the advantages of the warm weather and spend more leisure time outdoors with Andrew. We just knew that we were going to be very happy in Hong Kong.

Chapter 4 - Hong Kong

The week went in so quickly but I managed to visit the remainder of my units in the New Territories introducing myself and discussing the physical and recreational programmes required by the commanding Officers. I spent some time at Cassino Barracks with the 1st 10th Princess Mary's Own Gurkha Rifles and met the Officer Commanding the Rear Party as the Commanding Officer, Lt COL. McCready and the battalion were currently serving in Borneo. Further along the coast at Castle Peak, I visited 69 Gurkha Field Squadron Royal Engineers before calling in to 246 Gurkha Signal Squadron in Sek Kong; all made me very welcome.

Carmine had put Andrew's name down for a half day at the nursery in Sek Kong which would start in a few weeks' time when an army mini-bus bus would pick him up at Sui Pak Villa with a number of other children of army parents. 'I'll take him into visit the nursery and the swimming pool a number of times before he starts, and he can get to know the other children in the class.' she explained. 'They will all move up to class1 at the school together when the time comes.'

'Well done Carmine,' I replied, 'he will love it.'

Saturday arrived and we boarded the train to Kowloon and headed for Hong Kong Island on one of the very busy Star Ferries that crossed the Victoria Harbour continuously day and night taking approximately 10 minutes from the mainland to the Island.

In 1711 when some British merchants arrived and started successfully trading with a few fishing villages, they called the area Hong Kong and built a thriving trading port but trade declined and an opium trade was illegally introduced from India into China where the Emperor had banned its sale. This resulted in the Opium Wars (1838-1856) with China.

In 1842 Hong Kong became a British colony and in1898 a pact was formed with China which made Hong Kong, the surrounding islands and the New Territories up to the Chinese Border a British Protectorate to last 99 years. The treaty expired at midnight on the 30th June 1997 on the waterfront of Hong Kong when the Union Jack was lowered, folded and handed to the Governor Chris Patten. As the Black Watch led the British troops off the parade ground with some stirring music from their pipes and drums, there were not many dry eyes at the parade that evening and not only because of the heavy rain.

Victoria Harbour was one of the deepest in the world and was full of sea going vessels ranging in size from the huge American aircraft carriers to motorised sampans and Chinese junks filled with adults and their families, known as the boat people who lived on the junks and seemed to sail around the islands at will. There were passenger and tourist boats ploughing up and down, visiting the many surrounding islands including the Portuguese Island of Macau famous for its gambling casino. The many sea going vessels of various descriptions were monitored regularly by the Hong Kong Boat Police who somehow controlled and kept the flow of traffic moving, as well as intercepting illegal refugees from over the border; being aware of any suspicious craft entering the harbour area, stopping and searching accordingly. In 1962, thousands of refugees from Communist China had streamed across the border into Hong Kong. Little did I realise that in the near future, I would take part in the Annual Cross Harbour Swim Race.

Although the harbour was sheltered, all the small craft knew exactly where to head for when a monsoon was predicted and the fishing harbour of Aberdeen was one popular relatively safe anchorage. I had been told that the seafood in the Floating Restaurant in Aberdeen was very popular with locals and tourists alike and food on the menu was selected by pointing to one's choice as it swam around one of the large fish tanks; fresh as could be.

We stepped off the Star Ferry and followed the teeming crowds into the heart of Victoria. The noise of traffic ranging from lorries and trolley buses to taxis, rickshaws and bicycles was only superseded by the sound of high pitched voices rising from the hordes of local people and children crossing the busy roads, walking up and down the streets in every direction carrying from brief cases and school satchels, to poultry and bundles and packs of something or another. Somehow it all seemed to flow with everyone edging closer to their intended destinations.

'Do you think Carmine, that the next time we come to the Hong Kong, I will have the courage to drive through Kowloon, on to the ferry and bring the car over to the Island?'

There was a silence for a moment, Carmine looked at me, smiled and said, 'If you're not sure, I can always drive.'

'I fell for that one,' I said laughing but stretching my hand out at the surrounding traffic. 'We could drive around the island, picnicking on one of the beautiful beaches on the far side towards the market at Stanley nearby to Stanley Fort where currently there is a Welsh regiment occupying the barracks. We would love the warm sand between our toes and a good swim in the sea although I understand that jellyfish are fairly common and can give a nasty sting.'

'That sounds exciting,' replied Carmine, 'but I think we should gain our confidence on the streets of Kowloon first.'

'Of course you are right darling,' I said, taking Andrew's other hand to cross the street and head into the beating heart of Hong Kong.

Smart well-dressed uniformed policemen stood on pedestals in the centre of the road and conducted the traffic in all directions or mingled in pairs amongst the crowds. Their sand coloured shorts and shirts were neatly pressed with a small chain in their breast pocket portraying a whistle. The black shiny peaks of their caps were pulled down over their foreheads whilst on their belts hung a holster containing a standard issued pistol, handcuffs and a baton which were the hallmark of discipline and efficiency. Their gleaming boots, long dark stockings, black gaiters and sunglasses epitomised the cool look. The Officers of the police force were mainly British and wore Sam Brownes similar to officers in the British army.

Stalls selling huge varieties of commodities and

hot sizzling tempting food being cooked in woks of all sizes were ranged along the pavements with customers sitting on tiny stools eating rice or noodle dishes from bowls with chopsticks. Restaurants and bars had a continuous stream of people coming and going and often through the open doors the sound of customers clearing their throats and spitting into spittoons strategically placed would take a bit of getting used to.

The Peak was the highest point of the Island and we decided to take the funicular railway to the top to see the magnificent views and have something to eat and drink in the restaurant up there. Andrew nodded in agreement.

The steep climb in the carriage was amazing but the views of Hong Kong Island, the harbour, surrounding Islands, Kowloon and beyond to the New Territories were spectacular and breathtaking and we enjoyed the cool air on the Peak before entering the restaurant where the drinks and snacks were most welcomed.

Down in the centre amidst the teeming crowds, it was hot and we regularly bought and drank cold drinks as we wandered around the stalls and shops filled with ivory carvings, statuettes, trinkets, hats, Chinese fans, watches, lighters, souvenirs and every kind of commodity thinkable.

Sailors on leave from HMS Tamar mingled with American sailors and marines and all were mixing freely with the girls from the Wanchai District dressed in their traditional tight fitting cheung sarms. Many sailors made their way in pairs around the streets on rickshaws and some made their ways from one bar to another but Naval Police were patrolling and while there was lots of happy, laughing servicemen having their photographs taken in various poses there was no sign of trouble although the day was young.

Thank goodness we had taken a supply of sweat towels with us to mop our brows and looking at our watches we realised it was time to head back to the ferry crossing back to Kowloon. Crossing the harbour didn't take long and there were so much passing of vessels from start to finish on the journey that Andrew was as excited as we passed almost within touching distance of

31

the children on the junks. We were early for the train and like many other British families some of whom we recognised, we called into the YMCA for cold drinks and toasted tea cakes on our way over to the station.

By the time that the train pulled into Fanling, Andrew was sleeping and I had to carry him home the short distance to Sui Pak Villa. It had been a long but enjoyable day. Thank goodness for Sunday morning; no rush, breakfast on the balcony and a day in the garden with a few beers by the pool telling Arthur and Su of our first journey to the Island. Tommy and Andrew played all day in and around the pool.

I was settling in well at work and enjoying my responsibilities under my new boss QMSI (WO2) Ivan Goodwin whom I had known from Aldershot; he had flown out with his wife Connie and family, Gary and Tracey. Ivan had been the Swimming and Water Polo Specialist Instructor at the Army School of Physical Training and we decided almost immediately to form a Brigade water polo team to play in the Chinese League and swim in the Cross Harbour Race next year which would take a lot of training. Although we had the village pool for early morning training the choppy waves of the harbour was a different proposition; not to mention swimming around the anchored and moving boats, the dead dogs and anything else that had been tipped overboard and was floating on top of the water. Injections would be imperative.

It was about this time that I was selected to play rugby for the Brigade at the open wing forward position. We were playing a strong Welsh regimental team from Stanley Fort on a pitch in the centre of Hong Kong Island. The ground was a bit harder than back home but the match was going well for us when I tackled a huge Fijian player and as the side of my left ear caught his knee cap, I felt a tearing sensation before I blacked out.

'Are you okay?' I heard a voice asking. 'Are you able to sit up?' asked the referee pressing a pad against my ear and tying it with a bandage.

'I can see your lips moving but can't hear what you are saying,' I said

The team coach accompanied me to the British

Military Hospital not far from the pitch where my ear which had been hanging off was sewed back on with ten stitches. The bus with the team picked me up at the hospital at the end of the game which they said we had lost because I had left the pitch and should have stayed on even with one ear; I couldn't even laugh at their humour. I was delivered safely via Castle Peak back to Sui Pak Villa. When Carmine heard the coach and the cheering of the lads at the front gate, she got an even bigger cheer when she came out to see what the commotion was about. When she saw the bandage around my head she came running over to give me a hug and got an even bigger cheer. I assured her that I was fine and we waved the team off, back to Sek Kong. After a shower, some painkillers, a good night's sleep, a lot of sympathy and the following day off work, I was back in the office Friday morning.

Chapter 5 - Sek Kong

The weeks rolled by and before we knew it, we were celebrating Andrew's third birthday on the 22nd September. It was a lovely summer afternoon in the garden with our friends and their children, some who were at the nursery with Andrew.

In October Bruce Forsyth, the television personality who was visiting and performing in Hong Kong flew into Sek Kong in a helicopter to say hello to all the school children of the army personnel. What an enjoyable afternoon it was for the children and parents alike. Andrew had his photograph taken with him which made his mum's day.

In November I was informed that a quarter was now available in Sek Kong Village and although it was sad leaving Sui Pak Villa, we weren't leaving our friends; just moving a little bit further away from them although I would be seeing Arthur daily at the office. Su arranged a little farewell drinks and nibbles for us by the fountain in the garden and invited the amahs who all wanted to say farewell. Ah Cum was in tears cuddling Andrew and Carmine; I thought that we were going to have to take her with us. Tears all round but a lovely farewell.

We took over a beautiful two bed roomed red roofed bungalow in a small cul de sac at no.8 near the bottom of the village which had a main street stretching up a winding hill to the officer's quarters. We had a small front and back garden with a veranda and were now living at the hub of family life in the village with the school, swimming pool, cinema, family's NAFFI and relevant services on our doorstep. The camp, PT and recreational facilities, sergeant's mess, church, medical centre, airstrip and the HQ 48 Brigade Offices were less than two miles away. The airstrip had been built to evacuate British personnel in the event of an emergency such as China invading the Colony. Once a week usually on a Friday morning, an RAF plane would fly on a practice run on to the Sek Kong airstrip which because of the surrounding hills was quite a difficult approach. It didn't land, the wheels just touched the runway and it continued to take off with a great roar.

The Chinese traders from the shops around the village called at the quarters throughout the week selling everything that was saleable from fruits and varieties of food to made-to-measure clothes, shoes, cleaning materials, bamboo umbrellas and household gadgets. Anything required that they didn't have they would bring next time. Everything was carried in two baskets one either end of a long bamboo pole which was balanced across their shoulders. Fires were lit in the winter evenings and coal was carried in the baskets from door to door up the village hill. I tried one day to lift the pole with the two baskets filled with coal but I couldn't even lift it off the ground. The traders were generally small and slim with strong arms; their legs were like tree trunks, which wasn't surprising as they daily carried their wares up and down the steep hill of the village. They had a shuffling movement with their feet which was nicknamed the 'Shung Shui shuffle' (part of the Chinese shop area of the village that they came from). We always looked twice as we passed the meat hanging up on the trees to dry outside the shops.

From June to September there was the chance of a typhoon hitting the Colony, and when the weather forecast predicted one, junks, fishing boats and small craft headed for shelter to the nearest harbour. Around October to December, the monsoon season arrived and it was quite unbelievable how quickly the torrential rain poured down from the skies albeit for a few minutes causing the water to hurtle down through the monsoon ditches of the village, but before long the sun would be out again, beaming down on us and the umbrellas could be tucked away.

We settled into village life very quickly knowing almost everyone and having already made many friends. Selecting a new amah was a priority and ensuring that the one chosen would fit in with the whole family. There were no mod-cons in the quarters; no vacuum cleaner, nor washing machine; all clothes were washed daily in the bath. There was no dish washer or steam iron; shorts, shirts and uniforms were starched and pressed with a heavy iron. All floor mats had to be taken outside and shaken daily and floors tiles had to be polished and bumpered until gleaming whilst all brasses had to be kept clean with a continual shine. The guidelines and pay for an amah were generally of a standard nature. Our amah was called Ah Moi and had been recommended to us; she was cheery, trustworthy, and diligent in her work and patient with Andrew. She had her own amah's room for the odd sleepover if we were having a late night at the mess, and we liked her.

Social life in the sergeant's mess was good and we had become close friends with Mick and Irene Cox who lived in a nearby quarter. Mick was the Pay Sergeant at the Headquarters and was married to Irene a cheerful Malayan Chinese girl; their little girl Jeanette who could swim like a fish was in Andrew's nursery class and they had become good friends. With the nursery and primary schools on half days during the summer months, the swimming pool beside the NAFFI was a natural gathering place for mums and children where news could be discussed and spread quickly. Watching the children playing safely whilst sitting at tables under coloured brollies with a plentiful supply of cold drinks was indeed a relaxing pleasure. It wasn't long before Andrew had learnt to swim and keeping him out of the water wasn't easy but like everyone else, protection from the sun was imperative and sun tan lotion had to be applied regularly with hats being worn when out of the pool and sometimes even in the pool. The atmosphere in the village was friendly and the hot weather and spare time encouraged all to relax and enjoy life.

Village life compared to Kowloon was peaceful and friendly with an abundance of fresh air to breathe. It was always good at the end of a trip to Kowloon or Hong Kong Island to return whether by bus or car up the TWISK, past Tai Mo Shan and drop down into Sek Kong Village.

One sunny, Saturday morning, Ah Moi had gone up to the NAFFI to purchase some shopping when Carmine decided to hang out the washing on the line in the back garden with Andrew carrying the pegs. I was out in the front street washing the car and chatting to sergeant Geordie Smith, our neighbour from across the road, when we heard this shouting and screaming from the back garden. We looked at each other and nearly knocked down the Chinese street sweeper as I dropped the sponge and ran round the side of the house with Geordie and the sweeper right behind me.

Carmine was standing a few yards from the washing line pulling Andrew tightly into her skirt. I didn't have to ask what was wrong when I saw the two huge snakes coiled around the line basking in the morning sunshine. I grabbed Carmine and Andrew, and pulled them back but before I could take any further action, the sweeper stepped forward, gestured to Geordie to shut the back door and walked steadily towards the snakes. Holding his broom handle out, he gently nudged the two snakes that seemed to sit up and stare at him but he held his ground and nudged them again until they uncoiled from the line, slipped down the pole and slithered across the grass and underneath the wooden fence towards the bushes on the hillside.

We all sighed with relief before daring to burst out laughing. 'Ungoyli, dorgi', I said, to our new Chinese friend remembering the Cantonese for thank-you. He was smiling and bowing to us and although he held the palm of his hand up in a 'no thank you' gesture, I forced into his hand a few Hong Kong dollars that I happened to have in my pocket. He bowed, smiled again and with a wave of his hand, clutched his broom and went back to work as if it was all in a day's work.

Chapter 6 - Dashera

I had been kept busy visiting the units within the Brigade and especially with the oncoming Dashera (Hindu) Festival in October; I was training the children (nani) of 1st/6th Gurkhas over three to four weeks for the boy's gymnastic display team which would take place on the Friday evening, with dancing and other forms of entertainment. As young primary school children are, they were full of fun, always laughing and it was quite difficult to get them to co-ordinate their arms and legs, even doing forward and backward rolls. I decided to keep the movements simple but with lots of action and when I introduced vaulting over a gymnastic horse, the display rehearsals suddenly took on a new image; the problem was that they didn't want to stop and go home but I now felt confident that I would have the display ready for their big day.

For the Gurkha soldier, the Dashera Festival is the largest and most important festival of the year and celebrates the triumph of good over evil. It is divided into two parts; the main entertainment's on the Friday evening when the whole battalion attends and all are welcome including wives, families and invited guests. The Buffalo Service when animal sacrifices to appease the goddess Durga take place in the arena on the Saturday morning; only men and older boys are allowed to attend.

The Festival opens in the evening with a buffet and drinks for all guests in the marquee. The soldiers have their evening meal and indulge in beer and rum before finding a seat within the arena. After the meal and everyone is seated, an assortment of drummers tapping out a rhythm on the drums with their hands and musicians playing an assortment of pipes entered the arena. They were followed by a troupe of women dancers dressed in long saris, headdresses, bangles, ear and nose decorations, gyrating their hips in time to the hypnotic music. As they danced in front of the marquee and around the arena accompanied to the shouting of the soldiers who with their consumed drinks were in a happy mood and were entering the spirit of the festival; their cheers and clapping were loud and continuous. I didn't realise it until someone whispered in my ear that the women dancers were soldiers dressed up as women. It seemed that women were not allowed to perform in public at Dashera. They certainly fooled Carmine and me.

The dancers were followed by the children's gymnastic display which was a great success with the boys giving of their very best; tumbling on the mats, vaulting over the gymnastic horse with two teams crossing over and no one tripping or falling, no bumps or knocks and finishing with a huge cheer by the crowd especially from the proud parents. The Commanding Officer and the Gurkha Major came into the arena after the display and shook hands with all the boys and placed a garland of flowers around their necks. Seeing so many smiling, proud and happy children, I was nearly in tears myself when a garland of flowers was placed around my neck and the Gurkha Major shook my hand. 'Shabash, well done,' he said.

There was now traditional dancing from the soldiers themselves wearing white Nepalese styled shirts with matching pantaloons tied at the waist held up by a black cloth belt. They were in bear feet and a soft topi (hat) sat comfortably on their heads whilst displaying advanced skills and movements with their swirling kukris. The singing of Nepalese folk songs was popular with the audience who by this time had downed a few beers and more rum which seemed to help their vocal chords; they liked their rum which we would normally associate with the sea but I think that their monthly issue had a lot to do with that being a favourite tipple. When the Battalion Pipes and Drums entered the arena wearing their dark tartan trews, their plaids swirling behind them, everyone stood and applauded as the tunes from the Highlands of Scotland were carried around the arena on the light breeze; it was just like a performance that we had seen at the Edinburgh Military Tattoo a few years previously. The night was a great success and the evening was brought to a close with the soldiers, their wives and families; small children being carried starting off for home; having had a wonderful Dashera Festival.

The following morning, the arena for the Buffalo Service was packed with excited chattering Gurkha soldiers well before the arranged start to the proceedings at 1100hrs. Seats at the front were vacant for the Officers, VIPs and guests who included Ivan Goodwin and me. A young Gurkha captain who was a Queens Commissioned Officer (QCO) had been allocated a seat beside us to interpret the proceedings. A Q.C.O. was a British Military Commissioned Officer who had attended the Royal Military Academy, Sandhurst; a Queens Gurkha Officer (QGO) was commissioned through the ranks. The most senior Gurkha officer being respected by all was the Gurkha Major who was also commissioned through the ranks. The Commanding Officer and all other officers of a battalion were generally British and had been commissioned through Sandhurst.

A sound of bugles heralded the entrance of Cpl Dhansing Gurung dressed simply in white with a traditional red shawl around his shoulders who stepped out from the small tent where he had been living in almost isolation for the past six weeks. He was attended only by the High Priests of the Regiment who ensured that his meals were of the highest protein, his strength and fitness exercises were carried out daily, his stress levels were checked and kept low, his sleep was sound and undisturbed, his physical and mental state was ready to successfully carry out the task that he had been chosen for; nothing was left to chance. The good luck of the battalion for the whole year depended on him. He carried the huge silver sharpened kukri over his shoulder and he knew exactly what he had to do. The kukri was almost as tall as him.

About forty bleating and whimpering goats were led into the centre of the arena and were decapitated by various helpers wearing the white shirts and pantaloons with a red shawl around their shoulders and tied at the neck. The headless bodies of the goats were held by the back feet and dragged around the arena spreading blood and supposedly good luck everywhere.

There was a bellow of fear as the huge water buffalo smelt the blood as he was led into the arena. Eight assistants pulled the rope attached to the ring at his nose and two pulled his tail to stop him breaking free and stampeding around the arena. They were trying to walk him over to the tethering post in the centre of the arena but he wasn't going there easily. He froze, waved his head and tossed his huge horns from side to side as three other assistants prodded his haunches to keep him moving. The two aides pulling his tail deftly dodged the huge pile of droppings coming from the frightened beast. Inch by inch, the beast was cajoled forwards until the rope could be passed through the hole in the centre of the post and secured tightly around the post to the accompanying cheers of the crowd. Suddenly the excitement died down and a hush fell upon the crowd as the crucial moment approached.

The eight assistants stepped forward to pull the rope taut through the hole in the post and grip it tight as in a tug of war competition. Two assistants each pulled a hind leg backwards which had the effect of stretching the muscles of the shoulders and straining the thick leathery neck. Cpl Dhansing Gurung stepped forward to just above the shoulders and moved slightly to his right to stand level with the huge bulging neck with the huge kukri resting in his right hand. He bowed his head and closed his eyes. He knew that it was bad luck for the battalion in the oncoming year if he failed to cut the head off completely in the first downward sweep of the kukri. He had to get the angle exact between the neck and the shoulder; the downward sweep had to have the combination of strength and power with no hesitation of the mind and physical movement. He opened his eyes, raised the kukri above his head, held it still; took a deep breath and brought it down with an unleashed force slicing through sinew, muscle and bone. The huge head didn't move and there was a deathly hush from the crowd. The head swayed slightly before the knees buckled and the head rolled off the body and the once great beast crumbled to the ground amidst a spreading pool of thick red blood. It was good luck for the battalion and the cheers of the ecstatic soldiers who believed that good luck was required for the oncoming year.

The second buffalo was led into the arena wildly tossing its head as the smell of death crept up its black curling nostrils mingling with the heat and the flies. Once again the huge silver kukri sliced the buffalo's head from its body in one downward sweep splintering bone and sending blood spraying in all directions; the soldiers cheered and jumped up and down in a frenzy. Cpl. Dhansing had his head wrapped in swaddling bandages and was now anointed with oils and ceremoniously prepared to meet his Commanding officer. His broad shoulders and rippling biceps seemed to grow even bigger as the oils sunk into his body. When garlands were placed around his neck by the commanding Officer and Gurkha Major who congratulated him, he was hoisted shoulder high by the ceremonial aides and carried around the arena for all to applaud. How proud of him his parents back home in Nepal would be

The two huge heads were laid side by side with those heads of the previously sacrificed goats and all would be offered up by the priests to their Goddess Durga but the sounds and cries of the animals as they left this world and the smell of death conjure up a memory in my mind that I will never forget. As the arena emptied, a feeling of peace, confidence and happiness spread throughout the Regiment and this would be carried in the hearts of the riflemen as they prepared for active service in the sweltering jungles of Borneo.

Through a long standing custom, once a month wives and children queued up at the Quartermaster's Store with containers in their hands to receive the popular issue of rum that each Gurkha soldier was entitled to. Often it wasn't always consumed that night but saved up for special family occasions and celebrations such as Dashera.

Diwali, the Festival of Light was celebrated later in the month of October when homes and offices were illuminated by strings of coloured lights. There was a happy spirit within the battalion as various faiths and cultures mixed. Good natured gambling took place throughout the night and any rum that was left was shared out with Tiger and San Miguel beers but at all times there was a strong guard on duty around the camp who would have to wait until the following year to relax, attend and enjoy Diwali; their time would come.

Doreen and Ian Powell had two girls. Gail was ages with Andrew and Dawn was a little younger. They lived a few quarters away from Mick and Irene Cox near the bottom of the village and we had all become close friends. When Ian who was the Brigade Company Clerk gained his promotion to sergeant, it was beers all round in the mess at lunch time and a party for the families at the week-end.

As the days drew shorter and the winter nights crept in, our children began to think about nursery and school parties and what Santa Clause would bring them. Whilst Gurkha children enjoyed Dashera, our children enjoyed Christmas. Fires were lit in the evenings and our first Christmas in Hong Kong was nearly upon us.

Ivan had flown out to join the 1st Battalion 10th Gurkha Rifles in late 1965 on the last few months of their active service tour in Borneo before the 1st Bn.6th GR took over from them in the New Year. I now carried out Ivan's duties as the Brigade Training Warrant Officer Physical Training. It had been decided that I would join 1st 6th GR in Borneo in May/June of 1966

Children dancing at the Dashera Festival

Chapter 7 - Christmas at Sek Kong

The lifestyle in the village was peaceful, happy and enjoyable and with the amahs doing the household chores and the children at nursery, there was time for the ladies to partake in a personal choice of activities. When Carmine and Doreen Powell were offered vacant staff posts at the nursery they both agreed to accept and joined the staff. The hours were 0830 to 1230 hours Monday to Friday with the rest of each day left for taking up leisure and recreation of one's choice or just having a good old chat and a cool drink by the pool with friends.

We decided that on Saturday morning, we would drive down to Kowloon, do our Christmas shopping which Carmine was dying to do and treat ourselves to lunch in one of the hotels offering special Christmas lunches. We decided to have an early start and left the village about 9am, heading up the TWISK and down the other side of the mountain to Kowloon. Although early, it was warm and we had the car windows down. Andrew was strapped in and comfortable in the back seat and Carmine and I were in the middle of a conversation about how much we were enjoying life when suddenly the front wheels of the car went over something big followed by the rear wheels going up and over. We were shaken and jolted within the car. I applied the brakes and we screeched to a halt

'Are you alright Carmine?' I asked.

'I'm fine. What was that?' she asked, turning to check that Andrew was alright. I pulled into the side and opened my door carefully in case another car was coming down and around the bend; Hong Kong drove on the left and most cars were right hand drive as in UK. Lying on the road was a huge, dark coloured snake which looked about eight feet in length.

'Wow!' said Carmine as she came around the grass verge to the back of the car.

'It's come down through those trees,' I said pointing up the slope by the grass verge.

Carmine looked up in horror, ran back and shut

Andrew's door. 'Check the car Howard and let's go in case another one comes down that hill.'

I looked down at the snake; mesmerised at the size of it and was about to pull it on to the side of the road when it wriggled, came to life and slithered across the road as if continuing on its journey before the interruption. 'Hong Kong, it's that kind of place,' I remember mumbling to myself.

We drove on into Kowloon, parked in the Gun Club Barracks and decided to have coffee and find toilets before tackling the shops. As expected the street was crowded and we had just started our walk up Nathan Road when Carmine pointed to a sign outside the Mayfair Hotel that read morning coffee being served now. With the aroma of fresh coffee coming out of the front door to meet us, we were immediately enticed in. The coffee lounge was clean and comfortable, the staff wore very smart uniforms, morning rolls were offered with our coffee and the service was very slick. Andrew was fussed over by the young Chinese waitress. Again it was Carmine who spotted the sign announcing that 'lunch is served until 2pm; booking a table is recommended as it does get busy.'

'I suggest,' said Carmine 'that when we have finished our shopping, we come back here for something to eat before heading back to the car.'

'A great idea,' I replied and booked lunch for 1300 hrs. We wandered up one side of Nathan Road and down the other entering every shop that had the possibility of purchasing a Christmas present and even some that hadn't. Andrew was as fascinated by the toys in the shop windows and children in the doorways as we were by the cacophony of horns from cars and taxies. The smell of spices and varieties of food being cooked in the stalls by the side of the road filled the air as people walked or were taken in rickshaws to wherever they wanted to go

To ensure that they would arrive in time, we knew that our presents for home should have been posted by now but with our cards from the NAFFI, we would wrap them and post them within the next few days.

'I'm hungry,' said Andrew

'Me too,' I said

'Men!' said Carmine. 'Right lets head for lunch.' Laden with bags full of goods we made our way to the hotel which was on the left side of the road as we walked back towards the harbour with a welcomed breeze blowing in our faces.

The Dining Restaurant in the hotel was upstairs and the young waitress recognising us asked if we would like a table on the veranda which would be a bit cooler. I stepped outside and satisfied myself that Andrew couldn't climb and fall over the high railings. 'That would be lovely,' I said placing the bags down whilst admiring the view. The meal was excellent and Andrew and I finished with fruit and ice cream whilst Carmine had a meringue with butterscotch sauce.

I had just asked for the bill when it happened. Andrew who was standing beside the table decided to see what was happening in the street below, pushed his head through the railings and couldn't get it back out. Well we tried gently turning his head to the left, then right, pushing his ears in and pulling his head through to no avail. The manager tried rubbing some fat from the kitchen on to his ears while Carmine tried to console him. We were getting rather worried and considering calling a doctor or a policeman when a little voice called, 'I'm out Mum.' Sighs of relief could be heard throughout the restaurant and were accompanied by a round of applause. Everyone wanted to cuddle our little boy.

Back up the TWISK we drove and were so glad to reach Sek Kong and get home.

What a day!!

As most British Secondary School children attended boarding school in UK and flew out to join their parents during school holidays, special arrangements were made to have airline escorts travel with them. Younger children attended the primary schools nearest the unit that their parents were attached to. The children attending Sek Kong School put on a Christmas show which had a full house attendance for each of three nights followed by their class Christmas parties. Although there was no snow, the Christmas carols reminded parents of home and a few hankies could be seen wiping tears from the eyes of sobbing mums.

The Nursery school had their own party and Carmine, Doreen and the staff ensured that there was plenty of enticing food, lots of fun and games as well as presents from Santa. Burly Sam from the Signals Unit donned a wig, beard, red top and trousers with black wellington boots and made a wonderful Santa complete with his sack full of presents.

The Sergeant's Mess Entertainment's Committee decided to have a Christmas Ball and the dress would be mess kit with miniature medals to be worn. It was voted in by the members that Officers and their ladies were to be invited to the ball; they could only enter the Sergeant's mess through invitation. Other ranks below sergeant had their functions in the Other Ranks Club. Everyone was requested to enter into the spirit of the evening. One can purchase almost anything in tropical Hong Kong and from somewhere a Christmas tree was produced in the mess, decorated with holly, silver bells and a fairy on top. It was placed in the corner of the lounge creating a Christmas atmosphere as back home. A coach was laid on from the village and the surrounding area to allow everyone to relax and enjoy themselves without worrying about drink driving. A new Regimental Sergeant Major had arrived and the mess wanted to ensure a welcome for him and his wife. A dance band which had been formed from various military units in Kowloon was hired and the music of the evening kept the dance floor in full swing throughout the night. The buffet was superb and the Christmas Ball was a great success and enjoyed by all.

We celebrated New Year by inviting our friends and neighbours over, and 1966 was welcomed in with a traditional styled Scottish hogmanay; Mick Cox did the honours of our 'first foot'. A few well known songs were sung, some jokes were told, lots of food, beer and varieties of drink were consumed; oh! and a few wee drams of whisky. It was an evening full of fun and laughter shared with friends and a perfect ending to our first six months in Hong Kong.

A Kowloon market

Andrew prior to sticking his head in railings

A rickshaw ride
Kowloon

Chinese gardens

Day out in Chinese gardens

Andrew
Restaurant, Kowloon

1st day at school for Andrew

Andrew

Carmine, Andrew and Tommy at a party

Chapter 8 - Khud Race

In January 1st 6th GR left for Borneo leaving a rear party at Gallipoli Barracks. Time passed quickly and all units whether on the Island or up in the New Territories near the Chinese Border were involved with military training and taking part in sporting competitions ensuring that the morale of the regiments remained high.

As I had won the London District Welterweight Boxing Championships when I was in the Scots guards, I had the urge to try out my skills again here in the Far East. When the opportunity arose, I entered the Hong Kong Championships albeit up two categories to Middleweight 11stone 11lbs. I got down to some serious training combining it with cross country running. I had previously buckled my right ankle during a cross country race at my previous posting at Troon but a surgeon carried out a 'Watson Jones Operation' at the Princess Margaret Rose Orthopaedic Hospital in Edinburgh and was successful in strengthening the ankle joint. Running was a great asset towards my general fitness although I did have to wear a supporting strap on my ankle whenever taking part in running and jumping activities, more for confidence and peace of mind than anything else.

The most important training required for boxing along with shadow boxing, skipping, punch bag and pad work was sparring. I was fortunate that the Royal Artillery Regiment based in Sek Kong had some very promising boxers and I wasn't short of sparring partners. I was a natural southpaw which meant that I led with my right hand as opposed to an orthodox boxer who leads with his left hand.

The preliminary rounds were held in Kowloon and were well supported by the regiments stationed on the Island and around the New Territories. I had four contests and managed to win them all on points. What I hadn't realised was that I was now expected to fly down to Singapore and if I won there, take the train up to

Seremban in Malaya for the Far East semi-finals and finals. As I knew that there were some good boxers within the regiments in Singapore who had represented the Army back in UK, I didn't really foresee me travelling on to Malaya.

Carmine gave me all the support I could have wished for; 'Get down there and do your best to win,' she said. 'Andrew and I will be fine back here.'

I was looking forward to meeting some APTC friends down at the PT School in Tanglin Barracks in Singapore and to seeing how the physical training programmes were carried out down there. I had heard so much from instructors visiting Hong Kong about the available indoor and outdoor leisure and recreational facilities.

'Won't be too long,' I said as I hugged Andrew and kissed Carmine before jumping into the land rover.

'Take care and good luck.' she shouted as I blew a kiss, waved and headed for Kai Tak Airport.

In Singapore, I had two contests which I managed to win; again on points decisions. I said farewell to the staff at the PT School in Tanglin, checked my travel warrants, crossed the Causeway by coach at Johor Baharu and on up to Seremban in Malaya by train. I won my semifinal and had a day's rest before the Grand Final. Many of the officials were APTC Officers and instructors and had also travelled up from Singapore or from units within Malaya itself.

I wore a red sash and my opponent blue as per our corresponding corners. He was a corporal in the Royal Engineers who had represented the Army a few years before and when his right hook in the second round put me down on the canvas for a count of five, I knew that he was still a quality boxer. In the third round I was jabbing and scoring points with my right hand; realised that he was breathing heavy; the bell was approaching and I threw everything at him with hooks and uppercuts. When he leaned back on the ropes, I did catch him on his chin and to the side of his head but he covered up well and managed to stay on his feet until when the bell rang, he went down on one knee completely out of breath. His second crossed the ring, helped him up and back to his corner and sponged him down. The gloves were removed and we stood in the centre of the ring on either side of the referee awaiting the judge's scores to be read out by the Master of Ceremonies who announced that the winner was in the blue corner and the referee raised his hand. The scoring had been close but he was a worthy winner and as we shook hands I think that we both said something about hanging up our gloves. The following day, I had a look around Singapore before saying my farewells to all back at the PT School. I had an early night and a good night's sleep before boarding the plane the following morning. I had a silver medal and a boxing trophy in my rucksack and I was wondering what sport I could try next. I enjoyed the flight meal, sat back in my seat, closed my eyes and felt a smile cross my lips as I knew that I was homeward bound to Sek Kong.

Although I was still enjoying my training runs around the countryside we had now formed Brigade water polo and basketball teams and entered the Colony leagues. Both were sports which the Chinese civilians were very strong at and wherever we played, the competition was keen but we were always made very welcome and enjoyed the refreshments and banter afterwards.

I had been organising fitness programmes for the regiments and squadrons within 48 Brigade and swimming was a priority to ensure that soldiers would be confident and successfully manage in full battle kit, crossings of the fast flowing rivers of Borneo.

Because of military training commitments, the Brigade Khud Race (Hill race) was organised a little earlier in the year than usual and I decided prior to the race to try out the course accompanied by one of my Gurkha Assistant PT Instructors and experience for myself what a Khud race was really like. The accepted course for the race was the very high hill called 'Nameless' near Gallipoli Barracks. It was approximately 1 mile and 64 yards long and 1300 feet high, and I had been made aware of the steep upward slope and warned of the perilous descent.

L/Cpl Berobahadur, a Battalion runner had

volunteered to run with me and he grinned as we set our watches and he took off on the direct route that the runners would take; straight up the hill, heading for the top where on the day coloured markers would direct the route around a post to start the downward slope. Officials would stamp the back of each runner's hand as proof that he had ran around the post at the top of the course. I was so glad that we had chosen the early morning to run and I had decided that my tactics would be to tuck in behind Bero as he was nicknamed and stay with him up to the top. I was breathing heavy and my legs were telling me that I should take a rest but I knew that if I sat down, I'd be struggling to rise and start running again. I looked up and could see the top getting nearer. I looked again and couldn't believe my eyes; walking down the hill towards us were three Nepalese women with a group of young children. Each woman had a small child strapped to their backs. They spoke to Bero as he passed them and smiled and waved at me as they went off down the hill on a path just slightly off to the right. I thought that it was a mirage and wiped the sweat from my eyes with a wrist band but they were real.

'Are you alright staff?' asked Bero at the top. 'Do you want a rest?' he asked thinking of my welfare.

'No thanks,' I replied and took off downhill, heading for the finish line. I had only gone about 100 yards when a figure streaked past me; running, jumping, slipping and sliding on the loose stones and scree. I couldn't believe the speed that Bero shot past me with his flailing arms trying to co-ordinate his short stocky legs but his feet seemed to know exactly where to step and all without falling over once.

At the bottom Bero was waiting for me with a broad grin on his face. 'Shabash (well done) Staff, are you okay?' he asked as I fell over and lay panting on the grass. I signalled that I was fine and that I just needed a few moments to recover; In truth I thought that half an hour would be more realistic.

'What was your time Bero?'

'16 minutes 12 seconds,' he said.

'Well done,' I said as he pulled me up and I shook

his hand.

I think one day one of our runners will do it in about 15 minutes; one or two are not too far off it now', he said smiling with pride. '

'Did you see those wives with their children?' I asked

'That was my wife with our two children and the others were her sister and friend with their children. They wanted to see how a Scottish soldier would run and also give the lalabala (children) a walk.'

'Oh!' I said. 'Fantastic; tell them I am delighted to have met them.' I couldn't think what else to say except that I did wonder if with a bit of training they could make the team.

It was a warm dry day for the race, a large crowd of spectators had turned up and a record number of runners had entered. The units from the Island were well represented and judging from conversations heard some weeks previous to the race, the Welsh lads had some classy runners from their mountains and valleys not to mention one or two North of England fell runners. The competition looked keen and I was glad that I was helping to organise the event and not competing. The gun went off and 180 runners took off like greyhounds out off a trap. I noticed that the runners in the middle and at the back of the field seemed to be from the Gurkha regiments. It wasn't long before there was a long line of runners stretching up the hill and into the distance. Suddenly there was a shout as three runners appeared on the downward slope heading for the finishing line. Cpl Rambahadur Gurung 1/6th (Rear Party) came in first, followed by Sergeant Gyanendra Rai 1/10th and L/Cpl Sweeney of the Royal Army Medical Corps a close third. 'I've never seen anyone run downhill like that,' he said taking in deep breaths as he bent double; supporting his hands on his knees.

'I have,' I thought to myself.

The crowd gave a big cheer and a round of applause to all the runners as they crossed the line. There were refreshments for all who took part, presentations and a short speech by the Brigadier who said it had been an excellent event for all the units to have competed in.

The spirit of the competitors, the large crowd of spectators and the support of the families including their children, made the Khud Race an exciting day out for everyone.

Chapter 9 - Around Hong Kong

When the Sergeants Mess proposed a barbecue and evening sail to Lan Tau Island the coach was full and everyone with children knew that they would be safe and looked after by their amahs. The dress for gents was Hawaiian type shirts and slacks with ladies being given a free suitable choice. Everyone entered into the spirit of the evening and as the coach rolled over the TWISK and down to Kowloon harbour the chatter, laughter and even some singing from front to rear just never stopped. After the driver dropped us off, he drove over to the Gun Club Barracks where he would await our return sometime after midnight; he assured us that he would be waiting for us, and he was.

It was a warm balmy evening although most of the ladies had taken a light shoulder wrap in case it got breezy later on. The gang plank of the large ship was down; the skipper waiting at the top to greet us and as we boarded, we received our welcoming drink of bubbly; the engine was running and ready to go. The buffet table was laid out on deck with waitresses finalising the layout of plates and cutlery. The aroma from the barbecue tended by a chef wearing a tall white hat streamed towards us on the sounds of the background music provided by a trio dressed in Hawaiian style; the scene was set for a fairytale evening

Fairy lights twinkled as we glided out of Victoria Harbour towards Lan Tau and as the buffet and wines were being served, couples were already on the small upper deck dancing to the hypnotic musical rhythms as the boat glided into the night through the deep waters around Hong Kong.

'Are you happy?' I asked Carmine.

'Very,' she replied slipping her arm through mine

On the route back over the TWISK in the early hours of the morning, most ladies snuggled in to the supporting comfortable shoulders of their loved ones and nearly all eyes were closed as we rolled downhill into Sek Kong. Everyone agreed that it had been a wonderful night and at the next mess meeting, there was a resounding applause for the organising committee.

The following morning I was up early and slipped out of the house before Carmine and Andrew were awake. I wanted to see how the early morning training programmes that I had instigated twice a week were progressing throughout the Brigade and I was impressed by the activities that were being carried out at 1st 10th Gurkha Rifles. Riflemen, junior ranks, senior ranks, warrant officers and officers were running in combat kit, completing obstacle courses and carrying out physical training exercises including the fireman's lift where a simulated wounded comrade was carried at least a 100 yards. I had introduced close combat techniques as a form of self defence and that was proving to be very popular. All finished off with 15 minutes playing basketball or volleyball and a few words of encouragement from the officers to the riflemen of each Company. On dismissal, it was back to the barrack rooms for showers and into the dining hall or respective messes for baht at 0900 hrs.

'Will you join us in the mess for baht staff?' asked a Gurkha Sergeant Major

'I would love to, thank you very much,' I said. I knew that a mug of tea and a roll at reveille had been available to all but when breakfast came at 0900 hrs; they were more than ready for it.

'I'll just have a shower and meet you in the mess. Everyone knows you and will be delighted that you have joined us,' replied the Sergeant Major.

By the time I had chatted to the OC from Headquarter Company and walked over to the mess, the Mess Sergeant was at the door waiting to greet me.

'Ramro bhiyana (Good morning) Staff, (Ramaunu au bhitra) please come in.'

'Ramro bhiyana ,' I replied taking my beret off and hanging it up on a hat stand. I kept my official tracksuit top on with my APTC badge and chevrons on my arm as wearing my PT sleeveless vest in the mess would not have been etiquette. Those whom I hadn't met came up immediately to introduce themselves and welcome me.

'Ramaunu basno talo Staff,' (please sit down), said

Sergeant Jitbahadur Rai whom I now knew quite well from my previous visits to the mess. 'I hope that you will enjoy our breakfast.'

It was a help yourself from the hotplate, buffet meal and one could have as much as the large plate would hold. The baht (rice) was piping hot but I had to ask the Cook Cpl. what was sizzling away in the other dishes. 'This one Staff,' he said pointing 'is dumba, bhenro (mutton, sheep) and this one is bakra (goat's meat). Cooked in various juices.'

'Oh!' I said ladling a little of each on to the rice already on my plate. On the table were jugs of pani (water) and when asked if I would like some, I said 'just a little please,' and I thought the waiter looked twice at me but said nothing. Each place setting at the table had bananas and a number of raw green and red chillies laid out and I noticed that everyone around the table took a bite of mainly the red chillies before taking a spoonful from their chosen dish. I followed suit, bit into a piece of red chilli and swallowed a piece of goat's meat. It was delicious and I took another red chilli and devoured it with some rice. 'Very nice,' I thought to myself It was about now when I gave a rather irritable cough and cleared my throat that I became conscious that all around the table had stopped eating and were watching me. I could now feel my throat burning and tried to look calm and dignified as I gulped down my glass of water which was quickly refilled. I now realised that my face was red and all who were around the table burst out laughing. After a few more glasses of water, I recovered, wiped the tears from my eyes and tried to smile. I looked at my watch and gestured that I had to leave. As I left the mess, I waved and shouted 'dhaniyabad (thank-you) aru bida' (cheerio) and headed back to the office in Sek Kong checking before I went in that my face wasn't still red.

I had now decided to try 'The Gentle Way' which is what the art of Ju-do meant when it was thought about and introduced to the world as a sport by Professor Jigoro Kano all those years ago when teaching in Japan. I and a few others around the camp decided to invite a local Chinese Judo Instructor to start a class within the camp area and there was an immediate response of about thirty interested participants. Judo mats (tatami) had been issued a few years ago to the gymnasium but they had never been used other than for some general physical training but that was about to change. Mr. Wong Lun was the President of the Budokwan Judo Club based in Yuen Long in the New Territories and he brought some of his students already graded in coloured belts along to help us get our Sek Kong Club of the ground. We met on Wednesday evenings and enjoyed the judo from 1900hrs to 2100hrs followed by a few beers in the adjacent NAFFI.

After a few months, the first grading was held in July 1966 and involved demonstrations of basic throws, groundwork techniques, arm and choke locks and randori (competitions against each other). All the students of the club including myself were white belts 6th Kyu going for an upgrading to 5th Kyu yellow belt but two of us did well enough in all aspects of the grading that we were upgraded to 4th Kyu orange belt. I was now enjoying my new sport and was beginning to be able to assist new members who joined the club. I reached green and blue belts after some months but realised that if I did want to reach at least 1st Kyu brown belt, I would have to travel to Kowloon to join a flourishing club. The Chief Instructor of the Hong Kong Judokan was Sensei Iwami, a powerful Japanese 4th Dan black belt who had organised and trained his classes within the universities of Japan and had been invited to teach in Hong Kong.

He had a number of black belts from various countries training under him and that meant a serious 40 minute warm up of bending, stretching, competitive groundwork and uchi komi (individual techniques working under pressure, alternating attack and defence with a partner) before the coaching began. During coaching which lasted about 45minutes, talking was not allowed except between the Sensei and the student.

The last hour was for free contest practice (randori); changing competitors each time the gong was sounded. At the end of training time, the gong was sounded with three or four repetitive strikes and the cooling down session began by walking around the dojo and carrying out bending and stretching exercises. At the start of the evening, it was custom as a mark of respect to the Sensei that one removed shoes, stepped on to the mat and bowed. If it was a formal class, all would kneel together in front of the Sensei and bow when he called 'Rei' prior to 'Hajimi' (begin). At the end of the evening the class would finish again by bowing to the Sensei; Japanese customs were very formal and disciplined. I had reached 2nd Kyu blue belt when my request to join the club was accepted in the Spring of '67. In spite of the knocks and tired aching muscles I didn't realise then how much this new sport would affect my future in a way that I could never have dreamed of.

It was a sunny Saturday morning when Carmine, Andrew and I stopped at the old farming village of Cam Tin which was like stepping back into old China. The streets were very long and narrow with long red banners of Chinese writing hanging down either side of the doorways. Children were everywhere, running, jumping, standing or just sitting around eating bowls of rice with their chopsticks whilst water buffaloes plodded through the large pools of stagnant water chewing at grass, lying in loose piles. There weren't many men to be seen whilst some women were sitting on tiny stools, washing clothes in tin baths outside their front doors. Old ladies smoking pipes which had long stalks and very small bowls appeared in the dim doorways of the houses wearing traditional round straw Chinese hats with veils, loose fitting, black jackets and trousers. They were a perfect attraction for the tourist's camera but we had been advised that they didn't like having their photographs taken as they believed that their spirits would be taken away with the picture and that it was probably best not to stay too long.

We continued on to Yuen Long which had some modern shops and a Hong Kong and Shanghai Bank where our army wages were paid into. We withdrew some Hong Kong dollars and bought some fresh vegetables and bits and pieces for Monday's evening meal, and the three of us had an ice-cream before filling up the car with petrol, jumping in and heading up the

Castle Peak Road towards Kowloon.

We stopped at the beach where 69 Squadron Royal Engineers were based and I called in to say hello to some of the Assistant Physical Training instructors who were sunbathing, surfing and enjoying their time off with their families. We decided to have lunch and cold drinks at the 'Beach Cafe' and spend some time relaxing on the sands. Although we hadn't really planned it, we had thrown some towels into the car with our costumes and we all had a dip in the warm sea keeping a close watch out for jellyfish.

It was a lovely late warm afternoon and we decided that as to-morrow was Sunday and we didn't have to rise early, we would head on into Kowloon and have a look at the sights in the harbour. We sat for ages watching Chinese junks full of people and children sailing up and down the harbour as the Star Ferries ploughed across the harbour between Kowloon and the Island. Numerous other sea going vessels were either anchored in the middle of the harbour or were trying to find a passage through to wherever they were heading for. It was a wonderful sight and will always conjure up a picture in our minds when Carmine and I think about Hong Kong. I glanced at my watch and I knew that it was time to make our way up Nathan road through this other sea of traffic, up the TWISK and home to Sek Kong. Home and bliss!

Hong Kong

Junks
Aberdeen Harbour

Hakka women working in the paddy fields

Cobbler outside bungalow

Fruit seller at our bungalow door.

Fruit seller
Sek-Kong

Social in the Sergeants' Mess

Social in the Sergeants' Mess

1/6th Queen Elizabeths Own
Gurkha Rifles Pipe Band

Chapter 10 - Borneo

It was early May and I had been allocated a flight from Kai Tak with a small contingent of 1/6th Gurkhas who were flying out from the Rear Party to join the Battalion in Borneo. Leaving Carmine and Andrew in Sek Kong was not easy but I knew that Ivan and the staff at HQ 48 Brigade would be there to ensure their safety and be available if needed. I also knew how competent Carmine was and we had lots of friends in the village who would be seeing her daily.

We flew out to Singapore and on to Labuan where we boarded a motor launch to take us up river to Brunei. The long dark green landing craft wound its way up the swirling river to the accompanying chattering monkeys performing antics, cartwheels and somersaults, frontwards and backwards on the sandy beaches which ran up to the jungle on the eastern shore. The swarthy brown young QEO Nepalese soldiers aboard, looked serious, calm and brave as they held their rifles tight between their knees but ready for action if required.

HQ 51 Gurkha Infantry Brigade was located in Brunei with a Tactical Area of Responsibility Interior Residency of 4th and 5th Divisions in Sarawak, North Borneo (Sabah). Some time had passed before the minarets of the mosques of Brunei Town came into view. The Royal Corps of Transport Skipper berthed the craft alongside the short pier where a three ton truck was waiting to take us to our accommodation. It was now only a short flight onwards to the war zone in Sarawak, Borneo. As the Sultan of Brunei and his people were strict Muslims, alcohol was not allowed on the streets although bottles of beer were discretely sold in the small Sergeant's Mess.

Brunei Town was built on stilts which left the wooden houses rising upwards from the water where children were jumping off the swaying wooden bridges which linked the houses to one another; swimming, laughing and playing as if they were at the public baths. Fishing nets were hanging up to dry and being repaired as long narrow boats full of fish were paddled up and down the rows of houses. People were smiling and waving as they carried out their daily work and a feeling of happiness filled the air. Most of the men had nothing on but small hats, a coloured sarong from their waist to below their knees and the women had long dark hair with floral designs on their sarongs worn from under their arms to their ankles; all had bare feet.

We had to wait a couple of days on the plane arriving and although we were itching to get on with the journey, it was interesting to watch the families of Brunei in a whole new way of life at work and play. On the third day our small plane landed on the tiny airstrip and a young pilot with a broad moustache, smartly pressed light coloured Malaysian Airways trousers and matching short sleeve shirt with a Malaysian badge of wings above his left breast pocket was smiling and shouting 'Salam Pagee,' (greetings) as he waved us aboard; rucksacks and rifles were stacked in the small storage area and strapped down. The seats were arranged facing each other with the open cabin door through to the pilot and his assistant left ajar. The plane roared up the grass runway and almost immediately after take-off, turbulence buffeted the sides causing the Gurkhas to pull out their issued sick bags, bend over and deposit the contents of their stomachs into the bags.

The pilot who was sitting with one foot up on the instrument panel, smoking a large cigar, cap pushed back on his head looked into his mirror, smiled and gave me a thumbs up sign. The turbulence grew worse thrown up by the ridge of high mountains stretching out below and the Gurkhas looking very nervous and tense continued to look straight ahead as we were jostled from side to side.

Borneo is the oldest rainforest on earth and is home to the Orang Utang. Borac is the local rice beer drunk by the various tribes of Kelabits, Dyaks and Iban, probably introduced in past years by explorers and traders.

The plane flew above the tree tops of the vast areas of jungle and I began to worry in case the airstrip had been overgrown but suddenly like a beaming light there was a clearing and I could see below the small grass airstrip of Bario, a small hutted village deep in the jungle of Sarawak. Here under stretching camouflage nets amidst the dense foliage lay Headquarters. The pilot circled a couple of times testing the air thermals before commencing his run in on the flight path and it was truly a relief when the wheels of the plane touched down on the grass runway. I could hear an audible sigh of relief up and down the plane. The pilot circled and taxied back, coming to a halt at a small collection of bamboo huts with thatched roofs where I could see the Training Officer, Captain Henderson, the Gurkha Major and a small fatigue party waiting to greet us and help us unload our rucksacks, weapons, requested supplies and extra general baggage loaded at Brunei

'Sewa Salam,' (greetings) said the Gurkha Major. 'Good to see you staff. Kasto Cha?' (How are you)

'M Ramro Cha' (I am well) and it's good to be here with the regiment sir,' I replied as he shook my hand warmly.

'I see my riflemen are glad to have their feet back on the ground. I bet all the sick bags were used up on the plane,' he said laughing heartily.

'I don't think it's their favourite way of travel,' I replied smiling.

He laughed again as he turned to the fatigue party and gave them instruction to unload the supplies and deliver them over to the Quartermaster's stores where they could be checked and made ready for distribution to the awaiting companies in their jungle outposts. 'All weapons to the armoury now,' he ordered. 'Staff if you would hand your rifle into the armoury ASP. Dhaniyabad.' (Thank- you)

'You made it safely and good to have you with us staff,' said Captain Henderson. If you collect your kit, I'll take you over to your accommodation where I'm sure that you will find a cold drink and something to eat waiting for you. I'll see you after the evening meal and give you a quick pre-briefing before the 2/ic, Major Richards sees you in the morning after which you can familiarise yourself with the camp and the rules of safety and defence in the unlikely event of us being attacked.

79

Sgt. Jim Brewster, the REME Sergeant who lived close to us at Sek Kong met me at the front door of the rough wooden hut which was the accommodation where the warrant officers and senior ranks were sleeping. All senior and junior ranks ate in the same mess hut whilst riflemen ate in the cookhouse hut.

'It's great to see you Howard. You will sleep well and be warm tonight. I've switched your electric blanket on for you.'

I laughed and said, 'Good to see you all in one piece Jim.'

A wooden duck board was laid up the centre of the hut and to the left and right blankets were hung to act as doors and provide small spaces of privacy. Between each space which consisted of a bed, small table, a chair and a small chest of drawers hung blankets to give the effect of walls. Bedding was not required as personal sleeping bags were used. Glancing in as I passed the hanging blankets, I could see that most of the bunk spaces were at present empty (staff carrying out their duties somewhere) but all had some family photographs on display. A most welcomed bottle of an ice cold fizzy drink and a platter of sandwiches were on my table by the bed waiting for me with a bottle opener. I placed a photograph of Carmine and Andrew by my bedside.

'I suggest,' said Jim, 'that you climb out of your jungle greens and your boots, have a shower and jump into bed. I'll give you a shout around 1700hrs and I'll take you over to the mess hall and introduce you to those you haven't met. There are some naval helicopter pilots sharing our mess and they have some characters amongst them.'

'Great idea,' I said, as I remembered that I was now on active service and had to adapt to the required way of life. I looked forward to Captain Henderson's general briefing and updating of events to all senior members of staff later that evening.

The following morning, I was welcomed by Major Richards who explained that the Commanding Officer would see me as soon as he returned from visiting Delta Company and said how good it was to see me with the regiment and asked if I would attend a meeting at

1400hrs that afternoon. Within 24hrs of arriving at Bario, I was tasked with joining an observation patrol led by Lt. Wright to investigate reported sightings of Indonesian insurgents and set up a defensive ring for an SAS Patrol flying in by chopper to observe, confirm and take necessary action to quell any enemy confirmed movements.

The patrol cammed up (painted faces and hands dark green to blend with the jungle foliage), checked that each other's packs were secure, kukris and bayonets were carried on the hips, SLR (rifles) ammunition and magazines were at the ready and the operator had radio and antennae for communications when required. Each man knew exactly what his task involved as Lt Wright gave the signal to move out in single file. There were approximately twenty men in the patrol and a Kelabit tracker who took the lead as we moved out; all were quiet, alert, nervous but ready for action. I was number three in the patrol. Standard procedure was no smoking, no talking, no jingling of equipment, no knocking branches off trees that would signal to the enemy our direction of travel and no standing on twigs that would crackle and gave our position away to enemy patrols. Alertness at all times was crucial and immediate reaction to the patrol leader's signals was a must. At any sign of a small broken twig, a leaf fallen on to the track or a print of any kind the tracker would signal a halt to the man on point (out front) who would signal halt and crouch down; two riflemen would move out slowly right and left to cover the flanks. Progress was slow but alertness and preparation for an enemy attack was paramount.

I was surprised how hilly and dark in areas the jungle was and tracks often had to be climbed which were physically tiring as we carried our heavy packs and kept our weapons at the ready; sweat poured off us and sweat rags were a blessing. We rested with sentries posted and working in pairs ensured that one at all times remained alert when for example the other required the toilet. We ate a cold meal of hard tac (biscuits) and varieties of cooked curry or boiled mutton, fish and fruit from our compo rations. All tins and crumbs were carefully retrieved and placed back into the pouches of our packs; no trace was left for anyone passing to be aware of our presence. At the allotted time to move on, we quickly adjusted our gear, checked our weapons ensuring the safety catch was off, arranged our patrol positions, checked maps and compasses and moved off with our tracker leading the way.

After some gruelling approximately six hours of combating the heat and insects, we reached our grid reference and as directed by the Patrol Leader, sentries were posted in all directions to act as a warning against approaching enemy and a defensive ring was set up as the rest of the patrol started using their machetes to chop down vegetation and make a small circular clearing. All instructions were given by hand signals and when finished everyone was allocated a defensive position, remaining at the alert. After approximately two hours of waiting the now familiar sound of a helicopter could be heard high above the jungle canopy. A minute or so passed when the buzz of the rotating blades of the chopper could be heard and a dark shape could be seen hovering directly above the clearing. The branches of the trees were pressed downwards by the swirling blades and I waited with baited breath to see what would happen next.

Suddenly a figure attached to a winch through a clip and carrying a very large Bergen full of kit on his lap descended from the doorway of the chopper and slid to the ground. When he landed, he quickly undid the clip, picked up his pack, moved a few yards to the side and pulled out a map and was setting a bearing on his compass when another two figures, one after the other landed on the ground, checked their weapons and equipment, threw their packs up on to their backs and gave two hard tugs on the winch which was then pulled up. The sound of the helicopter had gone within seconds.

All three men were of average height, wore dark green bandanas on their heads and had beards. From their belts holding up their camouflage trousers hung machetes and grenades. Hanging across their chests were bandoliers of ammunition for their SLR rifles. Binoculars hung around the open necked loose fitting smock of the second man and the other had a small radio transmitter attached to his pack. All three were wearing high lacing jungle green boots and looked as if they had stepped out of the pages of a Boy's Adventure Annual and were ready for action. The leader raised his hand, gave a circular wave, followed by a thumbs up of thanks and all three members of the SAS stepped into the trees and disappeared. The whole action hadn't taken more than two minutes. We couldn't hide the clearing we had made but swept away all tracks and signs that would have given away our numbers and valuable information to the enemy. We moved away quickly disguising our direction of travel and leaving a rear guard cover against anyone who might follow. Our objective successfully completed, we now headed back to base by a different route from which we came.

The SAS patrol would be self-contained in tiny foxholes covered in jungle foliage for days and even weeks during which time, they would pass back to HQ valuable information of enemy sightings and movements. They would lie in complete silence in tiny fox holes, alternating rest and watching, gathering and recording enemy information or destroying enemies as required. All food receptacles and human waste were scooped into small plastic bags and carried out with them. Nothing at all was left as clues or information for the enemy. No doubt a similar action in getting them out safely was called for when their mission was complete.

Safely back at camp, Lt Wright thanked me for being part of his patrol and said that I had impressed the Gurkha Riflemen with the way I had conducted myself on my first active service role. 'Shabash (well done] Staff.' he said.

'Thank you for taking me along sir, it was certainly an experience.'

He shook my hand and stepped in to the office for his debriefing by the Battalion Intelligence Officer.

After a shower and a hearty meal, I said a prayer for safe guidance back and for the new experience that I had just gained; I felt good, closed my eyes and fell asleep thinking of Carmine and Andrew back in Sek Kong.

Chapter 11 - Stand To

The following day as I cut through the kitchen area, I heard a voice shouting 'Ramro din Staff. Casto cha?' and there was L/Cpl Chitabahadur standing on two empty ammunition boxes leaning over a large round metal container stirring boiling rice with an army shovel normally used for digging trenches and foxholes

'Ramro bhiyana (good morning) Chito,' I replied. 'I'm settling in fine. Good to see you.'

'Today is Sari gurum' (very hot).' he called. 'Be careful with the sun on your face and arms and always wear a shirt on your back and a hat on your head.'

'Dhaniyabad (Thank you) Chito, I will. Jai ram (Bye for now) Watch that Baht doesn't burn,' I shouted over my shoulder and as I went into the mess, I heard a hearty laugh behind me.

After breakfast, I organised some volleyball, football, a potted sports competition and some light circuit training to relieve the monotony for all who were not on duty. A window opened and a wave from the 2/IC summoned me over to his office.

'Good morning sir,' I said.

'Good morning staff, come on in. I'm told that you performed well on patrol. You impressed the riflemen. Well done.'

'Thank-you sir but I was in good hands and well looked after.'

'We have some supplies going out to Charlie Company to-morrow at 0900hrs and I thought that you might like to visit the Company. The navy pilot is flying a Wessex helicopter to the outpost and is carrying out some trial or another en route and would be delighted to have you along. Perhaps you could assist him in his trials. You will need your sleeping bag and kit for a 48 hour stay. Oh, I should explain to you about the exercise,' and just then the phone rang. 'The pilot will brief you,' he said changing the sentence as he picked up the phone.

'Thank-you sir, I'll be on board.' I shouted as I left

the room.

In spite of being careful, I did catch a bit of sunburn on my neck and arms and realised that I must never underestimate the Borneo sun. I had thought mistakenly that I was used to it from Hong Kong.

I had already met the Chief Petty Officer Pilot Harry in the mess and his assistant, Andy whose room was adjacent to mine. I drew up my SLR from the armoury, checked that my bayonet was secure on my hip, tucked my machete into its sheath and made my way over to the chopper which already had the engines started up. I could see Harry and Andy checking the fuel and ensuring that all the instruments were in working order, the radio was tuned in and that all safety and emergency equipment was present and stored where it should be. I placed my rucksack and rifle on board, looked around and waved to some of the Headquarter staff who were playing volleyball and jumped aboard. Andy placed a set of headphones on my head just in time for me to hear Harry say

'Good Morning, Howard.'

'Good Morning Harry. Thank you for taking me along.'

'You are very welcome,' he said with a strange smile on his face. 'I have to carry out an exercise en route finding a lost person at a location and assimilating a pickup of a patrol from a deep jungle rendezvous.'

'That's great,' I said. 'Who are we picking up?'

He looked at me, smiled that smile again; 'You!' he said. 'The 2/IC was going to explain to you.' It was then I remembered the phone ringing and my conversation with Maj. Richards being cut short.

'Nothing to worry about,' he said. 'I'll hover above the tree line and Andy will keep you right as you are lowered with your equipment by the winch to the ground.' It didn't seem too much to worry about and would certainly be a new experience for me. We flew over a dense carpet of green foliage above the tree line and after about half an hour, Andy gave me a thumbs up and slid open the door. I was secured to the winch with my equipment, SLR and rucksack and with a wave from Andy I was lowered through the trees to the ground. I released myself from the safety clip, gathered my wits about me and tugged twice on the winch to let Andy know that my feet were safe on terra firma. I looked upwards through the dark canopy in time to hear the swirling blades of the helicopter fading away. It had taken off without me and I realised that I was now on my own in the dense jungle; not a sound, not even chattering monkeys; just an eerie silence.

'What if he didn't come back or couldn't find me?' I asked myself. I had no flares, no map nor compass. 'If I ever met Harry again,' I thought to myself, 'I couldn't be held responsible for my actions. He just wouldn't know what hit him.' A little prayer helped me gather my wits about me and as I sat against the trunk of a huge tree, I pulled my rucksack closer, felt for my machete on my hip, reached for my SLR and loaded it with a magazine of live rounds. I wasn't going to be taken a prisoner quietly. I looked around and upwards; could see nothing; hear nothing; just sensed a lonely feeling of being abandoned whilst being watched. Imminent danger seemed to be all around. I now knew how Robinson Crusoe felt when he woke up on that lonely beach after being shipwrecked and saw a footprint.

After what seemed hours, I heard the low hum of the chopper and felt the downdraft of the swirling blades as the branches of the trees were pushed downwards towards where I was sitting. Suddenly the winch cable dropped down in front of me. I leapt to my feet feeling elated, clipped myself in, lifted my pack and my SLR and yanked the cable twice. As I was hauled up through the trees, I could see Andy sitting at the edge of the doorway waiting to pull me on board. Harry gave me a wave and in spite of feeling relieved that I wasn't going to have to make my new home in a tree house and live like Tarzan, I scowled at him. We peeled off and headed for Charlie Company. When we landed Harry quickly explained that he understood that the 2/IC had briefed me on the exercise of finding and picking up lost personnel from a nominated grid reference. I told him that he was forgiven but he owed me a beer when I got back to base camp.

A small clearing came into view and Harry

explained over the headphones that to avoid attracting the enemy, he would not be hanging about once we had landed. Rations, supplies and mail were unloaded whilst sacks of rubbish and confidential mail were taken on board to be returned to Bario. Captain Braithwaite stepped up from a dug out trench to welcome me, guide me through some barbed wire and down to the entrance of a small tunnel where I could leave my kit and would be sleeping that night.

'You will get used to ducking,' he said. 'That's another advantage our riflemen have in being short of height.'

I laughed and was glad that a sense of humour was around the trenches, tunnels and barbed wire.

'Two platoons are out following up information received from SAS patrols and Dyak Trackers. Our sentries are out at their posts and Sergeant Lalbahadur will take you around and show you the layout of the company including the tripwires, 'stand to' positions at 0400hrs, toilet facilities and wash areas. The password which is changed daily is required when incoming patrols are challenged especially in the dark; don't forget it or you may end up going back to HQ in a body bag.' The words reminded me that we were not just playing soldiers here as on a military exercise.

Riflemen who had recently returned from patrol were enjoying a mug of tea, some roti (bread) baht and kukhro (rice and chicken) in their mess tins and some sliced tarbuj (melon) as they were checking ,cleaning their weapons and kit before washing and having a sleep.

'Ramro din (good day) staff,' one shouted as he gave me a wave.

'Ramrod din,' I replied with a warm feeling of welcome surging through me.

'There are sentries around the perimeter and we must be careful moving around,' said Sgt Lalbahadur Thapa shaking my hand in a gesture of welcome. There are trip wires beyond the sentries to give them plenty of warning of approaching enemy patrols and there are warning strings from the sentries tied to one person's wrist at night in each sleeping area; he in turn would awaken all in that area and so the whole Company would be ready to deal with emergencies. I will show you your 'stand to' position which will be close to your large comfy bed that you will be sleeping in,' he said smiling at me.

'There's that sense of humour again,' I thought to myself

'At 0345 hrs, the duty piquet will awake you to be in position by 0400hrs. No alarm clocks allowed. Dawn is the likely time of any attack when men might well be asleep and unprepared. We won't and don't be late to get into position. Try not to even whisper, use hand signals and have a pee before you take up your position. OH! and do remember to bring your rifle with you. You are to remain at your post until the command 'stand down' is given.' I was aware of the importance of 'stand to' when defensive positions were taken up around the camp in preparation for an enemy attack.

'The latrine area is over there,' he said as he pointed with his chin in the direction of some poles with hessian around them, 'and always keep your weapon with you; a good tip is to tie it to your leg, then you won't leave it. No fires, or radios allowed and compo rations are to be heated on the small personal cookers inside the entrance of the tunnels and do eat plenty of fruit. Acquaint yourself with the camp but don't wander outside the defensive area, try to ensure that someone sees you or knows where you are at all times and keep your head down going below ground. Tick cha?' (Okay) he asked tipping his head to the right.

'Tick cha, ramro sangi (good friend) Dhaniyabad,' I replied appreciating the help and guidance.

Darkness crept in quickly and silently and that night, I slept on solid ground and lay underneath a firm shelf of earth 2-3 inches from my face. I had to stand in my sleeping bag and slip in and out of the three sided coffin sideways, dragging my rifle in beside me. I had brought a small torch, and even with a pin prick beam, it made a huge difference in being able to find things in the pitch darkness. I had washed all over my body as best as I could in the stream within the camp, had changed my socks but decided to sleep with my jungle boots on to avoid any embarrassment of not being able to find them in the blackness of the night at 'stand to'; never mind trying to get them on and laced up. I pulled my SLR close to me making sure that all rounds were in the magazine which I kept in the pouch on my belt designed for it; no rounds up the muzzle and I ensured that the safety catch of the rifle was on. I looped a piece of cord through the trigger guard and tied it around my ankle before slipping into my sleeping bag.; I was not going to lose my rifle at all costs. I knew that there were other bodies resting or sleeping close by but trying to relax underground and yet be ready immediately when called was not easy.

I was in a deep sleep when I felt my sleeping bag getting a firm shake and when I sat up, I banged my forehead on the earthen roof above my head. As I reacted by raising my left hand up to hold my head, I hit my new Seiko watch that Carmine had given me for our anniversary on the 22nd April against the roof and cracked the glass; the watch stopped ticking. I was mad at myself. I wriggled out of my sleeping bag and took up my allocated position, fitted my magazine full of rounds into my SLR and controlled my breathing; listening for instructions or sounds in the cold grey dawn. It was eerie and threatening; shadows seemed to be continually creeping towards us through the mists but I knew that quietness was a good sign. After some time, the sun started to rise spreading welcoming shafts of light through the trees and on to the ground. I wiggled my toes to keep awake and alert. My thoughts were rambling; and I was thinking of home when a tap on the shoulder informed me that the 'Stand To' was over. Breakfast and the daily routine of patrols, sentry duties, cleaning, checking weapons and equipment could now begin.

Two days later, I heard the helicopter coming in and was ready to climb aboard having said 'dhaniyabad and 'bida' (thanks and bye) to all. I was given a good sendoff judging by the waves and signals from the riflemen. I was glad to be leaving this highly dangerous situation but felt an inner pride of having spent time with some of the world's best soldiers and modest, simple people.

On climbing down from the chopper at Bario, I gave my report to the 2/IC who again thanked me for making an effort to be part of the regiment as he understood that it wasn't always easy to fit in with a platoon especially on active service.

'Well done Staff,' he said.

I felt good with an inner pride as I made my way over to my bunk. I was looking forward to a shower, a change of clothing and a spell of relaxation.

Chapter 12 - A Tragedy

One Morning, I had a free day and wandered down to the river and the dhobi (Old word from the Indian Army days) area where clothes were washed, rinsed out and hung up to dry which only took around fifteen to twenty minutes. I noticed that the home made shower that had been rigged up was vacant and selected that instead of the bath which was a very large old oil drum that one could fill with water by buckets from the river and climb into it, tipping in some soapy liquid and relaxing for the allocated time of ten minutes or fifteen if no one was waiting. One could always dip in the river but there were usually dirty sweaty clothes being washed and scrubbed in various detergents which were a bit off putting. There were always at least three sentries posted to cover this area and although safe there was no such thing as privacy. After completing my dhobi and hanging it up to dry, I enjoyed my shower, changed into clean tracksuit bottoms, a Physical Training Corps Vest, and army floppy jungle green hat; felt like a new man.

I made my way around the camp ensuring that the games and activities were in full swing and having a word with everyone that I met. I grabbed a mug of tea from the cookhouse and was feeling good as I made my way back to my bunk, wrote a letter to Carmine, closed my eyes and fell asleep. It was the growling sound of a low flying aircraft that awoke me and I realised that it was the Hercules overhead and that it was about to drop supplies on to the DZ (Dropping Zone) at the end of the runway. A large white cross and smoke canisters would act as markers and show clearly the strength of the wind and its direction for the pilot and his flight crew.

The difficulty for the pilot was to counter the turbulence affecting the huge plane whilst allowing for the wind to carry the gigantic bales of supplies as near as possible to the DZ and not into the river running parallel to the runway. The bales wrapped and secured in canvas would be pushed out of the enormous hold by the crew and there was always an element of luck attached to the drop. The system of recovery was, when all the bundles had landed and the signal given by the team leader, the fatigue party of around twenty local tribesmen who received some form of practical help at the village in return for their assistance, ran out of the safety area and on to the Dropping Zone where with a bit of luck, the supplies had landed. The bindings would be cut, the seals broken open and the enclosed stores carried up to the Quartermaster's compound. More than one run was usually required depending on the wind which could carry the bundles well off course. It was the last run off three and the plane banked and began its flight towards the DZ. Three little black specks appeared from the plane as the bundles tumbled to the ground. I looked up and was admiring the precision skills of the pilot when suddenly some excited porters ran out before the arranged signal was given. Onlookers shouted for them to come back. The team leader waved his arms and blew his whistle to attract them and although they stopped and looked up, they were rooted to the spot as though hypnotised as one huge bundle came closer and closer until, finally crashing down on top of the two leading men smothering them like a thick black quilt. Their screams were reduced to muffled sobs. Both men were still alive when the bundles were rolled off them and the medical staff had reached them but the next few hours saw them in such pain that death came as a relief.

I felt sick inside and a sadness swept through the camp for a couple of days but everyone knew that they had to keep their spirits up, remain alert at all times including when carrying out daily and routine duties. Tragedies had to and would be overcome.

Later that day, necessity made me pay a visit to the latrines which were divided by walls of hanging hessian. The toilets nicknamed thunder boxes were made of wood with a large hole in the centre; the contents were emptied and buried each day and some form of strong liquid disinfectant poured in to the hole. There was no roof and swarms of flies that were quite literally at home had to be swatted away before usage of the thunder box could commence. With the confined heat one could never acclimatise to the foul smell which discouraged sitting longer than required and privacy was not even a consideration. Any weapons that had to be taken in when usage of the toilet was required, had to have no rounds up the barrel, the safety catch on and to be secured normally with a piece of cord tied through the trigger guard and around one's ankle. I just hoped that there would never be an enemy attack when the latrines were in full use.

The Commanding Officer, Lt. Col. Hickey was now leaving the battalion and going home to UK on promotion and was being replaced by Lt. Col. McNaughton. Farewell celebrations were arranged at Bario with representatives from each company being flown in by chopper to be part of this very important event. Local dignitaries such as the Government Agent, his eldest son and their wives and families were invited. The Missionary who was also the Headmaster of the small school accepted the invitation on behalf of himself and his wife; they lived in a small hut on the river bank towards the end of the runway. Excitement was growing daily throughout the camp area and reached its zenith the day before the event when the battalion pipes and drums flew in from Singapore where they had been giving performances at Sungei Patani, the Gurkha Depot in Malaysia and around Singapore itself.

At 1500hrs, when they stepped out on to the grass area at Bario playing traditional Scottish tunes, they were immaculate in their white tunics and shorts, tartan plaids with tartan ribbons on the drones of the pipes rippling in the light breeze, white spats and their famous little black pill box hats; the crowd stood up and the welcome given was resounding. The audience was enthralled with the display of marching and Highland bagpipe music as taught at the Military Piping School at Edinburgh Castle and as performed at the Edinburgh Military Tattoo.

At the buffet, there was plenty of rice and varieties of curry for everyone and those off duty were allowed a can of beer or two. The sentries were doubled around the perimeter of the camp including the airstrip and beyond the river and there was no relaxation of security.

Colonel Hickey moved around chatting to everyone

whilst Colonel McNaughton stayed in the background unofficially meeting and saying hello to guests and members of the battalion, many who remembered him from a previous posting as a major and a Company Commander. At about 6pm everyone formed two lines facing each other as the two Colonels had garlands of flowers placed around their necks and walked up the middle of the line shaking hands with many old friends and receiving lots of best wishes. The pipe band played a number of slow melodic airs as Col Hickey was raised on to a homemade sedan chair and carried towards the officer's sleeping quarters when the band broke into 'Will Ye No Come Back Again' and a tear was visible rolling down his cheek. Col. McNaughton began thanking everyone for a lovely evening and bidding all a very good night. 'I look forward to seeing you at work by 0700hrs tomorrow morning.' he said with a smile on his face.

The days passed quickly with never a dull moment or sign of boredom. I visited each Company in their jungle encampments, spending at least two nights with them depending on the availability of the returning chopper; often meeting Jim the armourer en route to or flying back from a location where he had been checking or repairing weapons. Enemy sightings and movements kept all companies on the alert and sentries and trip wires were placed strategically around the outer perimeter of the camps. Patrols went out at irregular times and no mistakes were made with the daily password. One afternoon, the Malaysian Missionary Philip and his wife Maria came to see me with a message from the Chief of the Kelabit village who wanted to invite myself and some friends the following evening to the longhouse to meet his people and their families.

'That would be very nice,' I said. 'Would you please thank him and tell him that I would be delighted to come and bring some friends to visit his village.'

'Perhaps you would like to come for tea at our house first after which we will guide you down to the longhouse.' said Philip. 'Would 5pm suit you?'

'Great,' I said wondering whom I should take with me.

'See you tomorrow then,' said Maria.

'Look forward to it,' I replied and made a mental note to gain permission to visit the longhouse from the 2/IC who thought that the idea was good for fostering community relations with the local people but warned me that we shouldn't take any weapons nor ammunition with us for the obvious possibility of them going missing.

'Be back before midnight,' he said. I invited Harry, Andy and Jim along who were delighted with the invitation.

Philip and Maria were a young married couple, small of stature, with dark hair matching their dark skin and dressed simply in western styled clothes; he in slacks and a white shirt, she in a type of polo shirt and a light coloured skirt. Both wore sandals on their feet and crucifixes around their necks but their most striking features were their infectious smiles and welcoming body language. We were wearing jungle green uniform.

'Salam Pagee,' (welcome) called Philip extending his arms, cupping his hands together and bowing in a gesture of welcome as we approached his house by the river.

'Thank-you for inviting us to your home,' I said as I introduced my three friends. Two small oil lamps lit up their house and as we entered, I could see a table, surrounded by various types of chairs, a cooking area and another two doors that were probably a bathroom and a bedroom. The table was set with cups, saucers and three plates of mixed sandwiches and a plate of what looked like digestive biscuits.

'Please take a seat while I make the tea,' said Maria. 'I won't be a moment,' she said as she strolled over to the log fire where steam was pouring out of a large kettle

'Thank-you for coming,' said Philip. 'Maria and I have so much to ask you about the world.'

'Well I hope we can answer you,' replied Andy.

'I know that you will be able to enlighten us,' Philip said, looking at us with certainty in his words.

'Shall I pour?' asked Maria as she returned with a large clay teapot in her hand.

'Yes thanks,' we all said in unison, and she did.

'I'll say grace,' suggested Philip 'unless one of you would like to say the thanks to our Lord for this food on our table.'

After a second or two of silence, I suggested that Philip should say the grace and he did.

'Can I start by asking you what countries you come from? If you could tell us about your people at home, your customs; what you eat and drink and what you wear.'

'That won't take long for you Howard,' said Harry with a smirk on his face. 'Haggis, whisky and kilts.'

'What's haggis Howard?' asked Maria.

'Well,' I exclaimed, scowling at Harry.

'Do tell us,' said Andy with a straight face.

'I should have known when I invited the navy along,' I mumbled but the conversation had been opened up and the questions just kept coming.

'Did all Christians go to church and how were non-Christians treated? Was music played and hymns sung in the churches and was money collected at the services and where did it go to?'

'We have studied in Singapore but would one day like to visit the world especially Scotland and England,' said Maria. 'I hope that you don't mind us asking all these questions. I just have a few more.'

'Not at all,' replied Jim.

They asked about the children, the games and sports they played, schools and universities attended, methods of travel and communications. At this stage, Philip mentioned that it was starting to get dark and we should be on our way to the longhouse where the Chief would be waiting to greet us. We gave our thanks for their hospitality and Philip pointed out the track to the Kelabit Village. 'It's just over a mile from the camp,' he shouted as he and Maria waved us off.

'Keep on the track,' shouted Philip 'and I meant to tell you that they will be offended if you don't try the food that they offer,'

'Thanks we will,' I shouted as I looked over my shoulder and returned their wave.

'Well,' said Harry, 'let's go and see what's for supper.'

We looked at him and laughed.

Chapter 13 - The Kelabit People

The track was overhung with trees and hardly visible in the darkness which had crept in and around us. 'You lead the way Harry as you are the pilot,' I said.

'I'm only good up there above the trees,' he responded 'but I'll give it a go. Stay behind me and don't go stopping and disappearing for a pee or anything else. I'm not coming to find you in this jungle.'

'Right, one behind the other,' I said 'and let's go.'

We had only walked about 500yards when a bright piercing light shone directly on to us from a hill to our right and a voice shouted 'parkhinu.' (Halt). We froze, rooted to the spot, knowing that a machine gun would be pointed straight at us.

'Chinda chha!' (Identification)

'He wants to know who we are,' I said

'Well tell him before we're dead,' said Harry frantically

'M matrai bolnu siano Gurkhali,' (I only speak a little Gurkhali) 'Bolnu ahista ramaunu (speak slowly please), I said. 'Mero nam chha Staff Gee (my name is Staff Gee.) Physical Training. I have three friends with me; we have been invited to the gaon' (village)

'Chalan kuro?' (Password)

'Dasheria,' I said.

'Ramro' (good) Staff. Kasto Chha?' (How are you?)

'M ramro chha dhaniyabad,' (I am well thank-you)

'Thik chha bitnu (alright pass) Staff.' And the light went out.

It was frightening knowing that had we not known the password, we might have been shot dead where we stood.

'Well done Howard,' said Harry. 'Good lads these Gurkhas.'

I smiled and said, 'it was nothing.' We all laughed. Another 1300 yards approximately and the clearing with the longhouse came into sight. As we were about to cross the log bridge over the stream, near the entrance to the village, a group of tribesmen stepped out of the surrounding trees, carrying blow pipes with spears on top and long parangs (knives) hanging from a piece of cord tied around their waists which also held a quiver of long darts and a small bowel containing a poisoned liquid. The darts were dipped into the poison and lethally fired at whatever creatures were being hunted.

We stood still until one man who turned out to be the Village Chief held out his hand in a sign of peace. He gestured with a welcoming wave to follow him over the logs towards the longhouse which stood on stilts, dominating the clearing. Philip had explained to us earlier that all the families lived together in the longhouse which was not only their home but their school, religious centre, bartering area, meeting place and where all decisions by the village elders were made; in effect it was the village.

The Kelabit people were small in stature but stocky, swarthy brown in colour with tattoos on their bare chests and muscular arms, most of which were bound with arm bands of slim coiled rope. All wore a red coloured loin cloth but their striking features were their black hair which was round shaped on top like a monk with a straight fringe across the forehead. The large holes in the lobes of their ears were pulled down by the weight of the round heavy earrings which were placed in their ears when very young.

Around the Chief's neck hung a string of coloured beads and another of scraped white small bones. His face was an artist's dream with creases and lines which criss crossed over his flattish nose. His gnarled fingers on his left hand curled around his blowpipe whilst with his right hand, he pointed to the small gap in the hut about fifteen feet from the ground. He led the way up the long slanting log which had notches chipped away providing foot grips up to the entrance where a bamboo curtain hung. His bare feet seemed to stick to the log and with his crouching knees in front of his chest, he reminded me of an Australian Koala Bear. He reached the doorway and disappeared inside.

'Go on Howard, you're next,' said Harry 'and if there's anything funny going on behind that curtain, give us a shout.'

I was about to retort but the other members of the group were pointing up the log and gesturing to follow their chief and so I started my climb.

'I can give you a pull up if you get stuck Harry,' I shouted over my right shoulder.

'I'm Navy,' he shouted back as he started his climb. 'I've climbed many a rigging in my career.'

'I bet you were often tied to the mast and lashed for your impudence,' shouted Jim.

Harry tried to look back and nearly fell off the log causing a burst of laughter from those on the ground. He could be heard mumbling to himself as I pushed through the bamboo curtain into a still darkness; a hand touched my arm and guided me off to the side of the opening. As slivers of light pushed through the tiny gaps in the roof thatch and flames from the fires down the centre of the floor lit up the walls, my eyes gradually adjusted to the room as Harry came in through the curtain rubbing his eyes. Tempted as I was to say, 'Welcome, you are the next sacrifice,' I thought decorum should prevail and guided him over to where I had been standing.

A type of rattan matting ran down the length of the long house which was so long, I couldn't see the far wall. As coils of smoke curled up from the fires burning on large flat stones raised up from the floor and laid out at intervals down the centre of the room, a hole at the apex of the roof drew the long fingers of smoke upwards and out through the roof. Right and left of the centre flooring was a raised area with bamboo floors and dividing bamboo curtains denoting individual family living and sleeping areas where wives and children were sitting around and carrying out various tasks. The preparation for a meal seemed to be underway and food was being stirred and cooked in large pots on the shared central fires. The Chief beckoned us to take off our shoes and follow him down to where the house opened up into a large area where all the elders and the members of the village were sitting against the wall in a circle. We were divided and directed to sit at various points in the circle; I think to allow everyone to get a good look at us. As we sat down, everyone wanted to shake our hands and make us feel welcome. The Chief stood and said a few words during which the wives and children slipped into the room and joined the circle. Suddenly all broke out into a chant and with their actions, smiles and waving hands, we understood the welcoming gesture was for us and we did appreciate it.

We were then offered a drink in a large scooped out fruit similar to a melon which we were a bit dubious about but it tasted rather good; a bit like homemade beer although we nodded to each other just to be wary of drinking too much. Various fruits were passed around and as the men were singing and clapping the smell of roasted foods started reaching our nostrils. Dark meats and green vegetables were passed around in large leafs and we copied our hosts and started eating with our fingers trying to catch the juice as it fell from our mouths every time a bite was taken.

'It's good,' said Andy as juices were running down his chin.

'What do you think we're eating?' asked Harry.

'I'm not sure,' said Andy 'but it's really well cooked and different from anything that I've had before.'

I nudged the Chief whom I was sitting next to, pointed to my meat and shrugged my shoulders. He understood and spoke to two of the younger boys by the door who rose and disappeared out of the room. After less than a minute they were back carrying some items which they placed in the centre of the room. The room went quiet and we were horrified to see lying in front of us, a couple of different coloured monkeys with long tails, a wild pig and two squirrel like creature which could have been large rats.

I remembered Philip's words that they would be offended if we didn't try their food. 'Don't say anything. Just leave what you don't want to finish.' I said, looking at Andy who had gone a funny green colour. The two young lads demonstrated the hunt with blowpipes, tied the monkeys and the rat like creature by the tails and the pig by his feet to a pole and carried them out.

Suddenly, the whole house broke into raptures of laughter and we knew that it was our facial expressions that they were amused at. 'I'm going to the toilet,' said Jim and as he headed for the door. A man as directed by the Chief went out to show him the way. When Jim returned, he looked worse than when he went out.

'If you need a pee,' he said, 'go behind a tree; anything else, postpone until you get back to camp.' We got the message.

There was more singing and chanting from the hosts when the Chief indicated that we the guests should give a song. We had a quick discussion and decided on 'My Bonnie Lies Over the Ocean,' 'She'll Be Coming Round The Mountains' and Auld Lang Syne at which we got everyone to stand and interlock arms. It went down a treat. It was at this point that the Chief pointed to the high shelf running around the room where lots of packages were laid out on it. A semblance of a ladder was produced and some packages which looked like rolled up large banana leafs were lifted down and placed in front of the Chief. We were intrigued to see what lay within.

He carefully opened the parcels and unwrapped lairs of leaves, lifted out a small black skull from each package and held it out. Two men now stepped forward and faced each other with parangs as if in a mock battle. One man demonstrated how an arrow from his blowpipe killed the other and his head was severed by the parang, shrunk, dipped in a liquid and smoked over a fire to preserve it. Although headhunting had been banned in Borneo some years before, many trophies had been kept by the victors of the spoils in years gone by. He beckoned us forward to see the heads and a ceremonial chant broke out in the room. At the end of the chant, the heads were wrapped and placed back up on the shelf again.

It was time to leave and say thanks for a memorable evening. The Chief insisted that a guide take us back along the track to the camp for which we were very grateful. Some distance along the track, the light came on and once again, we froze.

'Chinda chha' (identify yourself)

'Staff Gee, Physical Training and friends,' I shouted.

'Chalan kuro?' (Password)

'Dashera'

'Thik chha bitnu Staff.' (Pass)

'Dhaniyabad', I called and the light went out.

'Well done again Howard,' said Jim. 'It's a good job that the army is here. I don't think anyone will get passed these checkpoints without identification being checked.'

'There are others even further out from the perimeter.' I said. 'It's a straight walk in to camp now,' I pointed in the direction of the track and turned to thank our tracker who nodded, smiled, raised his hands in a sign of goodwill, waved and was gone as if by magic. Back at the camp, we confirmed that none of us had any ill feelings from the food we ate or the liquid, we drank. All agreed that it had been a good night and one that we would always remember.

'First up in the morning should check that the other three were awake and well,' suggested Harry.

'Agreed,' we all shouted. I think we all slept soundly that night.

The Battalion's tour of active service in Borneo was coming to an end and they were preparing to handover to 1/7th Gurkha Rifles. I went round to say farewell to Philip and Maria and other locals that I had met. I said cheerio to Harry and Andy and we wished each other the best of luck. We had formed a good friendship in unusual circumstances with humour and banter between the army and navy and some good laugh over a few beers. I knew that I would see Jim back at Gallipoli but he was going home on a different flight from me and we shook hands wishing each other a safe journey, knowing that we would meet in Sek Kong.

I was very moved when I was presented with an inscribed kukri from the Commanding Officer and riflemen of the Regiment and treasure it to this day.

I gave Chiko our friendly little monkey some peanuts and a friendly pat on his head; he would be cared for by the team from 1/7th when they arrived. The journey home through Brunei, Labuan, Singapore and on to Hong Kong was full of memories but it was the greatest feeling of all when I stepped off the coach at Sek Kong and shouted 'Bida' (good-bye) to all those khushi (cheerful) faces waving and shouting back to me

'Dhaniyabad Staff, aru ramro bhag' (Thank-you Staff and good luck)

I knew that I had an inner feeling of being part of a team with loyalty and comradeship; I returned their waves as the coach rolled down the hill on its way to Gallipoli Barracks. I turned into our street, walked through the door and just can't describe my feelings of happiness through tears as I swept Andrew into my arms and cuddled Carmine both of whom I had missed so much. I was home.

Oh and I was given a new Seiko watch by the jeweller when he heard my story.

Feeding Chiko on my shoulder
Borneo

Member of the Kelabit tribe out hunting
Sarawak

Going home from Borneo

Chapter 14 - Dragon Boat Festival

After a few days of most enjoyable leave with my family, I was back visiting all my units preparing and assisting in their participation of fitness programmes, swimming lessons, teaching and coaching various sports and recreational activities. I was now in serious training for my brown belt in judo, playing in the Brigade water polo and rugby teams as well as training for the oncoming cross country season.

One day the Brigade Major asked me if I knew anything about the Dragon Boat Races which were to take place in about eight week's time.

All sorts of things went through my head but I said, 'No sir, but I'm keen to learn.'

He laughed. 'I think we all are staff,' he said. 'The Brigadier would like us to organise a team which should include some Gurkhas for the race which is held each year in July at a large Dragon Boat Festival held in the fishing village of Tai Po. It seems in previous years we have been knocked out in the preliminary rounds or have even sunk.'

'Sunk?' I asked with a look of amazement on my face thinking of British pride.

'Don't worry staff; it seems that there is always a safety boat on hand. The word is that we could have been sabotaged; all a bit of fun by the locals if you take my meaning'

'Surely not,' I thought to myself. 'How many are in the team sir?'

'About twenty; any size, height or weight. They are long boats for paddling with a dragon's head carved on the front and a tail on the back. The Brigadier wants to be at the helm and I am booking my place holding the Headquarter Flag at the centre and banging the gong to keep everyone paddling in time or as near as possible. The distance in the early rounds is about 6oo hundred yards and co-ordination of paddles and strength with a will to win will be crucial.'

'How many teams take part?' I asked.

'Oh lots,' he replied. 'Various Army and Service units, Police, International Traders Hospital and Medical staff and of course the Hong Kong people themselves who have been winning it for years and are the masters of speed paddling in teams. Huge crowds turn out to support their local teams and I'm sure we can organise transport for our wives and families to enjoy a day out and provide us with some encouragement. We will need all the support we can muster. Usually the organisers manage to arrange good weather,' he said smiling 'and a day of fun is predicted. What do you think Staff?'

'Sounds like a good event to win and fun for us all with the families sir.'

'Well that's great staff. I'll leave it all in your hands but keep me posted about your team selection and any problems that might develop.'

There was no shortage of volunteers and as boats were drawn by lots on the day, training wasn't really possible and all selected were advised to get fit and any help required for strengthening arms and shoulders could be organised through me. All who were selected were to draw up from the sports store a pair of white shorts and a white vest with the HQ 48 Gurkha Infantry Brigade badge sewn on to the front. Well I thought if we didn't win we had a chance of being the smartest team taking part. I was kept busy selecting the team, the reserves and trying to roughly work out who would sit with whom and at which end of the boat (front or back); trying to work out a balanced seating plan. I think the main concern was that we didn't make a fool of ourselves on the day but did have an enjoyable day out with the families. The big day arrived and it was hot and sunny. The families from the village were excited and all prepared for a picnic day out. The atmosphere was one of fun and excitement; being a Saturday there was no school and the coach which rolled out of Sek Kong as if it was a Sunday School Picnic. The team went in its own coach to ensure that all arrived at the same place at the same time.

We sorted out our seat positions and before we knew it, we were being called over the Tannoy to take our place at the start line; the flag was waved and we were off. At first we seemed to be veering to the left but once we settled down and started paddling straight and the Brigadier got the hang of the rudder, we were going strong and crossed the finishing line in third place out of seven. We were struggling to get our breath back when it was announced that we were going through to the next round. We were enthralled and managed to wave to all our wives and loyal children supporters sitting in a section of the crowd waving small Union Jacks. There were numerous other races and it was obvious that the serious competition was from the local Chinese teams who seemed to paddle as one; every movement in unison driving their boat yards ahead of their striving rivals at every stroke.

Amidst the firecrackers and general celebrations, we were called back on to the start line with five other teams, three who were Chinese and one Army Royal Engineers team from Hong Kong Island. The flag was dropped and we all went off like greyhounds out of a trap. The Brigade Major was banging his gong and shouting at the top of his voice and the Brigadier was using both hands to guide the rudder in one direction before switching to the other. We were paddling our hearts out when we suddenly realised that we weren't going anywhere except downwards; water was coming into the boat; we were sinking. 'Had we been sabotaged again?' I quietly asked myself. We tried bailing out to no effect and the order was given to 'jump ship.' The safety boat picked us up as the other four teams paddled furiously to the finishing line. We received a big cheer from the crowd and the Brigadier thanked us all for taking part; with tongue in cheek he commented that he hoped next year we would draw a boat that wouldn't sink. Boats were provided by the Tai Po Festival Committee. After a good laugh, a few beers and loads of food, we enjoyed the warmth of the sun, the atmosphere and had a great day out with the children enjoying the stalls and various entertainments.

Carmine and I decided to have a maritime weekend and on the following day, we drove down to Kowloon, crossed to the Island and boarded the hydrofoil to the Portuguese Island of Macau which was situated just off the coast of mainland China. Carmine had again prepared a picnic and it was a lovely warm morning when we set off over the TWISK. The hydrofoil was a new experience for us and with a fresh welcomed breeze in our faces we sat back and enjoyed the feeling of skimming over the top of the waves. The journey was under the hour and as we approached Macau, the Magnificent Cathedral standing at the top of a huge flight of stairs dominated the island. On landing, the first objective was to find the public toilets for Andrew and me.

We decided against dragging Andrew around the Cathedral and viewed the famous casino from the outside; people with serious money travelled from around the world to boast that they had rolled the dice and played at the tables there. We walked around the shops and stalls and had a ride on a rickshaw before dropping down to the beach for our picnic. After a few hours of playing, exploring the rocks with Andrew and relaxing in the sunshine, we again walked around the stalls buying one or two items of memorabilia before climbing aboard the hydrofoil for the return journey.

To and from Macau we passed lots of Chinese sampans and junks full of happy, smiling, waving children, who were sometimes hanging off the side of the boat fishing, washing clothes, washing themselves or even doing the toilet. It was a most enjoyable and interesting journey but it had been a long day and Andrew was sound asleep by the time we reached Sek Kong. After all we had done a lot that day; travelled by car to Kowloon, boarded a ferry to Hong Kong Island, experienced a hydrofoil to Macau, travelled on a rickshaw, walked around Macau and did it all again going home.

The previous year (1965), Ivan and I had entered the Cross Harbour Race. Although we finished the race, it proved to be a difficult experience with approximately 800 swimmers, huge waves and American warships not to mention Chinese junks in the middle of the harbour. This year we were determined to get some serious training in and try to gain positions much further down the field.

I was now training hard at judo and was determined to be awarded my 1st Kyu brown belt when I joined the Hong Kong Judokan Club in the New Year.

So much was happening and time was rolling by so quickly, probably because we were enjoying life so much. Andrew was enjoying nursery and had lots of chums in the village. Carmine had many friends and was involved in various activities. Social life in the mess was hectic with fancy dress dances, summer balls, games nights, Chinese supper evenings, themed dances, Christmas parties for the children and New Year dinner dances for the adults. Having an amah meant no problems arranging baby sitters which meant that all parents could go out, relax and enjoy themselves. Army life is very structured and provides work, housing and a social life which in many ways is a combination of its own community and family; one that people can drift in or out of.

Although we missed our families back home, we were happy and enjoying life in Hong Kong.

Dragon boat race
Howard left at rear of the boat

Chapter 15 - The Cross Harbour Race

With our early morning swimming training at the village pool, Ivan and I were determined to do better in the competition than we did last year and in August, we posted our entry forms off to the organising body and received confirmation of entry accordingly.

On Sunday the 18th September, with our supporting families, we made our way down to the starting point at Kowloon Harbour. It was a warm sunny morning but the water across to the Island 1600 yards away looked very choppy and there seemed to be more junks than ever ploughing backwards and forwards across the harbour, not to mention a huge American Aircraft Carrier and ships bringing in troops from Vietnam on R&R (Rest and Recuperation).

Police motor launches had given out relevant information, placed visible markers out and would clear the water in front of the swimmers but it did look daunting watching the endless sea going vessels ploughing through the waves where we were about to go swimming. We had been given our anti sea sick tablets and inoculations against contacting a whole host of maladies and advised that if we see any unusual flotsam such as dead dogs, try to swim around them or at least push them aside; not much we could do about the jellyfish and their stings. Goggles were a must and we hoped that our training would ensure that we would climb out safely when we reached the Island. All competitors hoped that they wouldn't have to be plucked out of the water for such as cramp by the safety boat. Carmine and the other families took the Star Ferry over to the other side to meet us at the finish line; hopefully as we climbed out of the water.

As we lined up on the pier, there seemed to be about 1000 swimmers of every age, sex, size and nationality although Chinese were obviously dominant;

all waiting for the gun to go off and when it did the brave competitors at the front of the pier dived in whilst the more sensible swimmers followed on by jumping in. At first there was a continuous bumping and pushing of bodies but our tactics was to adjust to the cold water, swim through the crush, settle down into our front crawl at a steady pace and try to up the stroke count per. minute when we felt physically ready; ignoring the jelly fish. I was about half way across when I turned my head to the right took a gulp of fresh air and my hand grasped a soft furry bundle of something and I automatically pushed it away. I stopped and peered through my goggles but couldn't see a thing. I heard a voice behind me shout, 'come on mate, you can't stop for a pee here,' I laughed to myself and started swimming, determined to catch up on the seconds lost but I did wonder what I had shaken hands with. I felt strong and was doing well but there were lots of bodies in front of me and all around me; judging by the sounds and noises that they were making, quite a few were either being sick or strangled by creatures surfacing from the deep. I hadn't been mown down by a Chinese junk yet and at long last I could see the crowds of people waiting on the pier ahead but they didn't seem to be getting any closer. I spluttered a bit, swallowed a little water and hoped that my life wouldn't end with weird water bugs swimming around inside me but there was nothing I could do. I decided to try and pass a few of the swimmers in front and increased the speed of my arm and feet action and felt good as I moved through some very tired swimmers. At last I crossed the Finish Line which lay between two speed boats and walked up to the recording tables. I was so pleased to have finished and absolutely thrilled to have been placed number 140 which was 55 places better than the previous year. I had no idea what my time was although the first swimmers to finish were around the 19 to 20 minutes but the real good factor was that Ivan finished 11th; what an achievement out of a 1000 swimmers. I was met by Andrew and Carmine who had a large towel and a hot drink ready for me.

Around the finish area, we met up with colleagues, friends and their families, had a good blether and shared all the news about our various units which were spread throughout the Island and the New Territories. Some had decided to spend the day shopping or driving around Hong Kong but after some thought we decided to head back over the TWISK and spend the remainder of the day at home. What an exciting day it had been; finishing the race by reaching the Island in spite of the choppy seas, shaking hands with a furry monster from the deep, jelly fish, Chinese junks and whatever had been tossed overboard from them; memories that would last were tucked away. We had met many friends from units all over the Island and the New Territories and had a good blether with them. It had been a happy, fun day out and one to remember but once again it felt good to get home to the peace and quiet of Sek Kong.

HQ 48 Brigade in the New Territories had been asked if they could assist every second Saturday throughout the summer months in providing security personnel for the Hong Kong Jockey Club at the Happy Valley Horse Racing Course situated on the Island. Personnel stationed on the Island would cover every other Saturday. The dress would be uniform to ensure that those selected stood out from the huge crowds of spectators. The main tasks involved would be informing the civilian stewards of any problems or trouble that might arise such as pickpockets, thefts or people trying to get entry without tickets. We had to leave approximately at 1130hrs to ensure that we arrived by coach, had a sandwich lunch and were in position around the gates by 1330 hrs. The pay was approximately over a 150 HK dollars, working until approximately 1700hrs and home by about 1830hrs. Ivan took on the task of organising the personnel including available Gurkha soldiers with myself as his deputy. Very seldom was there any trouble and if there was, the Stewards and Hong Kong police had it all quickly in hand. We enjoyed the atmosphere of the races, a coach there and back, lunch and we were well paid for it. The experience was enjoyed by all and there was no shortage of volunteers.

Inter regimental and company sports of all kinds from football, rugby, basketball, water polo, volleyball, athletics, and swimming were taking place throughout

Hong Kong and Ivan and I were kept busy at 48 Brigade organising competitions, teaching swimming and participating ourselves in the Brigade water polo, basketball rugby and football teams. Leagues and knock out cup competitions in most sports were well catered for and participation was high and very keen. I was training for the oncoming cross country competitions and was determined to be fit for my oncoming judo grading.

When requested to organise a swimming gala for Gurkha soldiers at Inter Company level, we knew that the standard of swimming would not be very high but the competitive spirit would be out of this world and it was. We organised the competition at the Sek Kong pool and throughout the day, it was packed with competitors and their jahan (families). The lalabala (children) were very excited throughout the day especially at the promise of being allowed into the pool at the end of the gala. The event started early at 0900 hours and the races which were all relay races to encourage as many to take part as possible were going well but the officials were ready for and delighted when a short break for lunch was called.

After the lunch break and a few more heats of various races, it was time for the final of the 4x25 meters breast stroke and the seven teams lined up at the shallow end where all the races started and finished. The whistle went and all the swimmers dived or jumped in and swam as hard as they could towards the deep end where the second man in the team was waiting for the incoming swimmer to touch the pool with both hands before he could enter the water. In lane four the number two swimmer going in at the deep end was fidgeting about rather nervously but when the incoming swimmer in his lane touched the end slightly ahead of the others, he jumped in with an almighty splash; arms and legs flailing in the water. Amidst all the excitement at the changeover it wasn't immediately apparent that Rifleman Prakish Limbu hadn't surfaced. One of our Chinese lifeguards nicknamed Lofty dived in pulled Prakish off the bottom and swam back to the side where he was quickly pulled out and on to the side choking and spluttering water everywhere. When Prakish stood up taking huge intakes of air into his lungs Lofty received a huge cheer and a standing ovation from the crowd. The gala continued with no other emergencies and was a very successful day which ended with all the lalabala (children) who could swim jumping into the shallow end of the pool but closely monitored by the Chinese lifesavers.

I made my way over to ensure that Prakash was alright and to ask what had happened

'One of my team took cramp in a previous race and couldn't swim in the breaststroke team. I was told to take his place.' he said.

'Yes,' I said waiting for the follow up to the explanation.

'I can't swim Staff but I am on the next course with you'

'Did you tell your team leader that you couldn't swim?'

'No Staff, I was told to take Lokendra Limbu's place and that's what I had to do.'

What could I say? In many ways that summed the Gurkha soldier up; he didn't question the command given to him by his senior; he merely tried to do his best.

Once again, the annual typhoon winds and monsoon rains had swept through Hong Kong, sweeping down the village street of Sek Kong and filling the ditches with thunderous roaring water flowing down from the heights Tai Mo Shan. Bamboo brollies were cheap but invaluable and no one went anywhere without a brolly. The temperature was changing, Chinese coolies were selling and delivering coal throughout the married quarters, fires were burning in the hearths throwing out welcoming warmth at the end of a working day. December was easing its way in to the calendar. Nativity Plays were being rehearsed at school with children's parties providing the excitement for the young families. Sergeant's Mess dances and social evenings were being organised regularly whilst fun nights with our friends, either at our home or theirs provided a good laugh and lots of fun. It was a happy atmosphere throughout the Village as Christmas and the 1967 New Year heralded in eighteen months in Hong Kong.

Chapter 16 - Start of another Year

A special service celebrating Christmas for all denominations was held at the Brigade Church and all the pews were filled. Although families at home were missed, it was a wonderful time with lots of happy children, toys, Santa Clause, carols, presents, Christmas trees, holly, mistletoe, food and drink, and although we didn't have snow, the atmosphere in the village was as a winter's fairyland.

The 1967 New Year came in with a bang when the clocks struck midnight and fireworks went off throughout the village. Drams were poured from numerous bottles of Scottish whisky with toasts of good health drunk to everyone including our families back home.

The battalion football teams were starting their training for the Nepal Cup which all Gurkha Regiments throughout the Far East took part in; it was very prestigious to win and the inter regimental rivalry was fierce. Ivan and I were officiating and coaching various sports including basketball and athletics whilst organising and teaching at swimming classes as well as refereeing at inter regimental boxing competitions. We had to travel around the units stationed in the Colony; from the Queens Regiment based in Gun Club Hill Barracks, Kowloon to the South Wales Borderers followed by The Welch Regiment based at Stanley Fort on the Island. We were also playing for the Brigade Team at basketball and water polo.

I was training hard for judo and my cross country running ensured that I was building and keeping my stamina up. Often when running over the hills I would come across gravestones in small community graveyards with no boundary fence or wall and I had to quickly change my route but there was sometimes remnants of joss sticks (sticks of incense which gave off a sweet smell when burnt); fruit and other small personal mementoes were left beside them in respect for the deceased.

The Qingming Tradition that was observed on or

near the 5th of April stretched back into Chinese history for over 2500 years. It was a Holiday and Festival occasion when Chinese families could reunite with their ancestors, remembering their deceased family members and honouring their spirits. Whole families, young and old visited the graves to worship, sweep the area around the graves and clean the stones. Joss sticks were burnt, firecrackers were lit while food and imitation money and paper gifts were offered and left at the graveside. Picnics including the popular rice cakes were eaten around the gravestones and a good family day out was generally enjoyed by all.

The Chinese people were very superstitious about all sorts of things and deciding the best design of a building was extremely important. Large new buildings were being built throughout Hong Kong and the Chinese art of Feng Shui was used regularly in order to bring good luck to that building and all who worked or lived within.

The 22nd April was our 6th Wedding Anniversary and we decided to invite a few friends round for a Chinese Mandarin style meal cooked by our amah, Ah Moi, assisted by her friend. Ian and Doreen Powell, Mick and Irene Cox and Pete and Beatrice Gregory brought over enough drink to last well into the early hours of the morning. We had a wonderful evening with jokes and humour from Mick and although not always very melodious or harmonious, we sang songs and choruses in between laughing and drinking throughout the evening. Andrew slept through it all but it was a good job the following day was a Saturday.

On Monday morning I called into the Headquarters to check the mail before I drove round to Cassino Lines where the 2nd King Edward V11's Own Gurkha Rifles (The Sirmoor Rifles) had taken over from the 1st 10th Princess Mary's Own Gurkha Rifles to see if my Fitness Training programmes were going well, and they were. The Commanding Officer Lt Col. ED Smith DSO MBE was delighted with the sports being played and encouraged within the battalion. He was keen that all his riflemen could swim and were confident in water hazards if having to traverse fast flowing rivers of which there were many in Borneo. He was exceptionally pleased with my efforts to speak in Gurkhali to his riflemen. Colonel Smith had lost an arm in previous times and was revered by all who knew him. It was not a surprise to the Regiment and the Brigade when he went on to a high ranking career.

When I was a Scots Guardsman, I served under Major Philipson, a Company Commander who had lost his leg in a car crash and had been fitted with a wooden leg which his batman could change according to his daily duties and requirements; he was also admired by all who served with him.

One Wednesday afternoon, the Commanding Officer 1st 6th, Lt Col. McNaughton asked me to pop in to his office to see him.

'Good afternoon Staff. Are you well and enjoying life? I know that you are very busy doing your rounds with the regiments and squadrons.' he said gesturing to me to take a seat.

'Good afternoon sir. I am well and very happy with life,' I said as I sat down on one of the large armchairs at the low hand carved, teak table; my feet inside my white PT shoes adjusted comfortably on a large eastern woven carpet. He flopped on to one of the other three matching chairs.

There was a knock on the door and Major Henderson held it open to allow a rifleman from the officer's mess to enter. He was dressed in dark trousers, a white waiter's jacket with matching gloves, carrying a silver teapot on a silver tray with cups, saucers, silver spoons and a silver cake stand on which lots of appetising fruit cakes were displayed.

'Come in Jamie, take a pew,' said the Colonel to Major Henderson.

'Thank-you sir. Good to see you staff,' he said shaking my hand. 'I've been hearing about the stalwart work that you and QMSI Goodwin have been carrying out around the Brigade.'

'That's good to hear sir and may I congratulate you on your promotion to Major,' I said smiling. 'A worthy promotion indeed,'

'I've heard about your sense of humour Staff but

thank-you anyway, I appreciate it.'

'Right let's get down to business gentlemen. Jamie would you do the honours please and pour the tea,' said Col McNaughton. 'Now Staff,' he continued. 'Have any of the other regiments requested your assistance in coaching their Nepal cup Team?'

'No sir,'

'Well Staff our team have voted for you as their first choice as coach and trainer. I hear on the grapevine that other battalions are planning to ask you also.'

'I would be honoured to work with 1st 6th sir and as a team we'll do our best to win.'

Major Henderson will be the Team Officer and as I'm sure you know, each team has to have a Commissioned Officer or a Queens Commissioned Officer (QCO, Sandhurst Military Academy Trained) playing in the team. Unfortunate for us Major Henderson is having to attend a Senior Officer's Course at Sandhurst and will be leaving the Battalion temporarily but he is being replaced by a young captain (QCO) whom I believe is a very useful football player. Major Henderson will give you all the help and support he can until he leaves.'

'When would you like training to start sir?'

'As soon as possible, the team have been selected and are ready to go.'

'I'll talk training times through with QMSI Goodwin and phone Major Henderson with details this afternoon.'

'Thank-you Staff and good luck,' said the Colonel. 'I'll follow the team's progress and pop down to the training ground as often as possible. Can you let yourself out and visit the Gurkha Major's office before leaving? He'd like to see you.'

'I can sir and thank-you for the tea. Oh! and the cakes were delicious.'

Chapter 17 - The Nepal Cup

The Gurkha Riflemen were by nature happy, honest, very loyal soldiers who loved their family traditions and Highland bagpipe music. They loved to compete in running up and down hills, take part in various sports and activities and play football, especially playing for or supporting their team in The Nepal Cup, a trophy for Gurkha Regiments

On my first training session, I had decided to watch and assess the team spirit, individual skills, the strengths and weaknesses of the team. I could see immediately at the warm up that there were characters and lots of spirit combined with a quiet confidence within the team. I divided the squad into groups, assessing their individual ball skills before regrouping forwards and backs. I watched the handling skills of the two goalkeepers and their bravery in going for the ball when my assistant trainers lobed successive balls into the goal area. After a short break, I continued with fitness and pressure training to ensure that all including the reserves were up to the skill and fitness standard that I was looking for to win the 1967 Nepal Cup for 1/6th GR. I knew that it was important to encourage team spirit within the squad

The following morning before training started, I gathered all twenty players in the squad around me and the two assistant trainers, who were also responsible for ensuring that the required footballs, coloured bibs, bottles of water, first aid kit etc were present and ready for use.

'Jati bhiyana,' (Good Morning), I shouted. 'Bhayana lai kath aru sutnu ramro?' (Early to bed and sleep well?). 'Nahi rakshi?' (No rum?).

'Jati bhiyana (Good morning) Staff. Ho, bhayana lai kath, nahi rakshi aru nahi mai' (yes early to bed, no rum and no woman). There was a brief pause as they all looked at me and burst out laughing. I smiled and shook my head.

'Right!' I said. 'Chamchum (quiet). Basnu tala' (Sit

down), I said, gesturing with both hands. 'We have a strong team of good players but we must want to win and play well on the day and I don't have to remind you of the importance of teamwork. Do you want to win the Nepal Cup?'

'Ho (Yes) staff,'

'Are you sure?'

'Jyu!, ho! (Yes, Yes) Staff,' they shouted as one.

'Ramro' (good), I replied. 'As you know Major Henderson has gone off on a long course and we are very fortunate to have Captain Akaising Thapa who is a fantastic footballer and will be team captain.' The team clapped and Birbahadur who was the administration clerk and team spokesman, said that they were delighted to have him as the team captain and that they all knew he was a great player. They unanimously welcomed him into the team with a rapturous applause.

Captain Akaising who was rather embarrassed said thank-you and promised that he would do his best to live up to the fantastic reputation that he deserved and would try to be a worthy member of the team and a good team captain.

I could sense the humour being bandied around and the spirit in which it was being given and received. The smiles and laughter said it all.

'Aktiyar,' (Right) I said, 'you have sat about long enough; on your feet and let's get warmed up. We'll start with a jog around the outside of the four pitches and no cutting corners. Janu!!' (Go)

After a good warm up and some stretching exercises, we moved on to ball skills; dribbling in and out of white poles and medicine balls, in pairs playing the ball but keeping it off the ground. In threes, piggy in the middle (small groups) passing whilst keeping the ball away from the man in the middle, various other games which required a skill factor with the ball. Relay races with and without a ball, skills in defense and skills in attack including the taking of corner kicks, free kicks and penalty kicks and deciding who would take them. Practising throwing the ball in from the side lines and having a shot at goal were all basic skills that I considered important and insisted that time was spent

125

on them.

The goalkeepers had their own skills to practice such as calling for the ball, catching the ball in the air from corners, left and right crosses not to mention from down the middle and from free kicks and penalties. It was also important that from our goal kicks the ball went to our team and not squandered by giving it away to the opposing team. When the ball was caught by the goalkeeper he had to hold it securely before throwing it out to our own team players. Punching the ball away was an important skill for a goalkeeper if he couldn't quite catch and hold it.

'Running into position to receive a pass, calling for the ball, spotting gaps in the defense were some of the many attributes of a good team.' I told them. Tackling hard but fair, not giving silly free kicks and certainly not penalties away; ensuring that you are not sleeping if your opponents are awarded a free kick and no speaking back to the referee. I don't want to see us ever down to 10 men because a player has been sent off and lastly, I want to see every player trying his hardest and performing at his best until the final whistle is blown. Of course it goes without saying that shaking hands with our opponents at the end of the game regardless of the score is important.'

'Garnu timiharu bujhnu thitos?' (Do you understand lads?)

'Ho, (Yes) Staff.'

'Shabash. Bato lai Jharis aile (Well done; off to the showers now) Dekhnu timiharu sabai boli.' (see you all tomorrow)

The team trained hard and it was no surprise when we won our first three matches in Hong Kong. We made ready to travel down to Singapore for the Quarter and Semi- finals, winning both matches. The team spirit was high, on and off the pitch and the journey passed quickly. The next stop was Sungei Patani, the Gurkha Depot in North Malaya for the Final. We travelled on the overnight train which had individual bunks with privacy curtains which allowed us to lie down and have a sleep. As the train slowed down and came to a halt, I peered out of the window into the station at Kuala Lumpa, the capital of Malaya. Enthusiastic, noisy vendors were walking up and down the platform selling varieties of food and drink to all who opened the train doors or thrust their heads and hands out of windows. I stayed awake and watched until the train snaked slowly out of the station in the morning mist and through K.L. northward bound.

We arrived a few days prior to the Final allowing us time to settle in and have some training days and talks on tactics. We knew that 1st 2nd King Edward VII's Own Gurkha Rifles (The Sirmoor Rifles) had a very strong team and were favourites to win but we were quietly confident and at half time the score of 1 goal each led us to believe we could do it. In the second half the team were magnificent and played their hearts out until the final whistle went but we lost the match by 2 goals to 1. Captain Akaising was an outstanding team captain and an example of the true Gurkha spirit. He encouraged the team to realise that they had tried their very best and that there was always next year to win the Nepal Cup but it was a long journey back to Hong Kong and our families.

Back home, trouble with serious riots had broken out at a cement factory in Kowloon. Industry and agriculture were badly disrupted and numerous, troublesome incidents had taken place; perhaps even orchestrated along the Chinese Border. The police did their best to cope with the situation but Mainland China had now threatened to invade the Colony and emergency plans were prepared for flying the families out of Sek Kong to Singapore. The Nepal Cup faded into the background as regiments on High Alert were rushed to defensive areas on the Chinese Border. All H M Forces were placed on stand-by for duties as required and the RAF were made ready at Sek Kong and Kai Tak Airport in Kowloon to fly out nominated personnel, if the decision was given

The situation was very tense but somehow the politicians in UK and perhaps the world, with the Governor of Hong Kong and his team, found answers to the problem and persuaded the Chinese Government to 'come to the table' where a peaceful solution was found and put into practice. A sigh of relief spread through the families at Sek Kong as with all servicemen throughout the New Territories, Kowloon and on the Island including the Navy and RAF personnel at HMS Tamar and Kai Tak.

What a relief to get back to a normal family life enjoying the warm sunshine and the ways Hong Kong.

Chapter 18 - A Super Star

Carmine and I awoke each morning and stepped out from under the mosquito nets to the sound of the swirling fans hanging down from the ceiling. Morning ablutions were carried out and at breakfast paludrine tablets to prevent malaria were swallowed. Andrew had now started at the village school, settled in, was enjoying the lessons and had lots of friends. He and Jeanette, the daughter of our friends Mick and Irene had become like the water babies in Charles Kingsley's famous story of that title. They were happy and had fun whenever they were in the pool; they had both become confident swimmers which we knew would be a great asset to them later in life. Carmine was enjoying life in the village and every day was involved with some activity or another with our friends in the village, by the pool, the NAAFI, or even down in Kowloon shopping.

As a 1st Kyu brown belt I had been training very hard at judo and had now received authority to travel with expenses to Tokyo in Japan with the aim of being awarded my 1st Dan black belt which was an opportunity that very few Europeans had. I was pleased and excited about the trip and was training very hard to ensure that when I reached the Kodokan, which was the centre of world judo where up to two or three hundred judoka trained in the dojos daily, I would hope to be able to hold my own in randori (free practice contest sessions) without getting injured which would jeopardise my chances of passing my black belt examination. I was travelling down to Kowloon every Wednesday night, sometimes arriving back home around1130pm.

The news spread fast around the Colony that Isao Inokuma, the World and Olympic Heavyweight Judo Champion had arrived from Tokyo to conduct a 10 day judo clinic for advanced students in Hong Kong and I had been invited to attend. His trip was at the invitation of Takeo Iwami, the sensei (Instructor) of the Hong Kong Judokan.

Inokuma-san won the All Japan Judo Title in 1959

and in 1960. He also won the World Judo Title and the Olympic Heavyweight crown in 1964 and was currently an instructor at the Kodokan. When he stepped off the plane at Kai Tak Airport, he was a magnificent picture of a man, about five feet ten inches in height and about the same in width, smartly dressed in a dark suit and matching tie. He wore a constant smile on his face which seemed contrary to his thick cauliflower ears; his whole aura shouted out 'do not mess with me.' The journalists from the local newspapers were out in force looking for a statement from and photographs of this Japanese hero. At the dojo (judo hall) that night it was again packed with members of the press and judo brown and black belts including myself who had travelled from all over the Colony to report on or have a coaching session under Isao Inokuma.

Etiquette was very important in judo and having removed one's footwear, a judoka (judo player) would step on to the tatami (mats) and bow as a mark of respect to the sensei (instructor) and other players on the mat. Before randori (free contest practice) both players would bow to each other and when the gong was sounded to change partners, they would again bow. In a formal class session, all would kneel facing the sensei who would also be kneeling and at his command of 'rei' all students would bow to the sensei who would return the bow; their heads would be almost touching the tatami. In a match contest, each competitor would bow to the referee and to each other before the command from the referee 'hajime' (begin) would start the contest; at the end of which each would bow again to the referee and each other; before shaking hands regardless of the decision.

At the end of the Samurai Era, the carrying of weapons was banned by the government but to protect themselves from roving bandits, travelling monks took up forms of defence which didn't require weapons, such as karate and judo (Ju – Do, the peaceful way) remaining within the law.

Grades in judo were introduced by Professor of Physical Education Jigoro Kano in the early twentieth century and children, women and men could take part in the sport of judo for fun, enjoyment and exercise whilst developing a healthy mind and body as well as a competitive spirit.

The senior gradings were from brown belt 1st Kyu upwards to black belt 1st Dan and upwards through the black belt grades. International competitors had mostly gained their 4th Dan black belts in contests whilst Grade 5 to 7 were awarded by Judo Committees for past successes in National or International competitions. When Isao Inokuma shook off his straw sandals and stepped on to the mat wearing a red and white 9th Dan belt (8th and 9th were red and white belts), a silence swept around the dojo. Very few people outside Japan had seen such a high grade and applause broke out throughout the dojo. The ultimate highest grade was a red belt 10th Dan which is the same colour as a very beginner; a full circle having been completed.

Inokuma's specialty throw was Tai Otoshi (body drop) and on most occasions when he manoeuvred his opponent into position through deft skill, they were thrown with power and speed on to their backs for a full ippon (full point and contest won). On the mat, he bowed, accepted the round of applause and announced that he would do some demonstration throws for the journalists before starting the Clinic, 'if I can find a willing partner,' he said smiling and pointing at me. I think that Iwami sensei had told him that I was coming over to the Kodokan later that year. For the next 10 minutes while cameras flashed, I was thrown and landed all over the tatami with various spectacular throws such as Harai Goshi (hip sweep), Ippon Seoi Nage (one arm back throw) and Sasae Tsuri Komi Ashi (lifting pull throw) but I managed to keep picking myself up knowing that I would be able to tell the lads back at Sek Kong that I had been thrown more than once by a World and Olympic Heavyweight Champion. For the next 10 nights the dojo was full and students had to wait to get on to the mat for randori by a continuous changeover system, signalled by the gong and controlled by Iwami sensei. The coaching sessions and Ouchi Komi (practice techniques) throws, holds, choke and arm locks were beyond what we as students could have learnt in such a short period of time at our normal classes. The sweat poured out of us and the drinking water machine was refilled at least twice. The time passed so quickly and although physically we were all pleased when the gong went for the end of training and winding down exercises to begin, I'm sure that we would have stayed on until the wee hours of the morning or until we dropped through sheer exhaustion had we been asked to do so.

Isao Inokuma was mobbed by the public as he was taken around Hong Kong daily to see the sights and sign autographs. He was indeed a Super Star. He thanked me for assisting him with his demonstrations and promised to come and see me in Tokyo.

One Saturday afternoon, Andrew was playing up the hill at the back of the quarters with a few pals; it was a safe area for them to play. Carmine was busy around the house and I was washing the car when Ah Moi the amah came in all red and flustered

'Missy, Missy,' she shouted, trying to explain the situation in her best English, 'my friend has just told me that Andrew and some boys are up the hill throwing handfuls of earth and grass down on to some family huts and I think there are some graves on that hill also.' I dropped my sponge and following Ah Moi's pointing finger raced up the hill. Andrew was in the middle of a crowd of boys who froze when they saw me. There were about eight of them, and Andrew and Paul, one of our neighbour's boys, looked the youngest; the rest looked about six or seven years of age

'Right boys what's going on'? I said. 'Are you all OK?'

'Oh hello Mr Gee,' said Robert, the tallest lad a bit sheepish with a divot in his hand which he let slip to the ground. 'We are all OK and have not been causing any trouble,'

'Andrew are you alright?'

'Yes dad,' he replied a bit embarrassed that I had turned up.

'Right then we'll start again. Robert, tell me what's going on?'

'Well,' he began and before he could say another word an angry looking, local Chinese villager came striding up from the huts towards us, waving his arms and shouting in Cantonese what seemed to be rather unpleasant words. Just while I was thinking of a way to defuse the situation, a voice from behind me shouted out, again in Cantonese. The man slowed down his approach and stopped a few yards in front of me.

Ah Moi, held up her hand in a sign of 'hold it and wait there,' to the man. She then turned to the boys, asked them what had happened and listened as they related their story after which she turned to the villager and asked him why he was so upset. She heard his story that the boys had ran over his family's grave kicking up the bones of his ancestors; then started throwing divots of grass down on to his home.

Ah Moi then explained to the man what the boys had told her and their story was that they had come up the hill, running, playing and rolling around on the grass when they saw a number of large birds crowding over what they thought was a dead animal. They ran shouting and waving their arms chasing the birds away. They found two large vases which had been toppled over but still containing long burnt out joss sticks; the grass around the grave stone had been dug up leaving some bones lying on the surface.

'The next thing was your dogs started barking and although they were behind a fence, the boys didn't want to run in case you let them out and they were attacked and may have been bitten. They then thought if they threw some divots of grass at the fence, the dogs would be scared and stop barking. They were worried in case you thought that they had caused the damage to your grave and they are very sorry that you have been upset.'

'I think,' she continued, 'that the typhoon a few days ago uncovered the surface of the grave and the birds did the rest of the damage. I also think that your ancestors would understand what happened and I'm sure that you will be able to bury their bones and allow them to rest in peace. Perhaps you could say some peaceful prayers, a blessing, light some new joss sticks and find family happiness for the future. I'm sure that you will find peace for yourself and your family again.'

She signaled to the boys and they altogether said

'Sorry.'

The man's attitude changed, he smiled and stepped forward, gave a wave to all the boys, turned to shake hands with myself and nodding his head, he said 'Ungoyli' (thank-you). He faced Ah Moi, clasped both her hands in his and said 'Dorgi,' (a more formal thank-you) and with a wave, turned and went down to his home presumably to fetch a spade.

'Well boys,' I said 'let that be a lesson to you to be careful where you are walking in future. Tell your mums and dads the story and if they want to pop down to see me, I'll explain everything to them. Off you go down the hill and keep out of mischief.'

'Ah Moi, you were fantastic. I think you should have been a diplomat. I'm so glad that you can speak the language.'

'So am I,' she said laughing. 'I think I should put the kettle on and make a pot of tea.'

Chapter 19 - Sunshine on the Water

Everyone in the village knew everyone who lived in and around the village, and sun loungers in the gardens under the multi coloured brollies were the place for the ladies to meet as a change from the pool area. There they would sip afternoon tea or cool drinks with biscuits and rice cakes being tended to by the amahs whilst they relaxed and enjoyed a quiet peaceful time catching up with all the local news. It was hot, very humid, and cold drinks, sweat towels fans and sun glasses were a must whilst shorts or even beach wear could be worn by choice. Whatever the dress the chatter with friends was not affected; enjoying the tranquil social life of Hong Kong was the order of the day. Men of course had to go to work. In general however life was restful and peaceful unless one travelled down to Kowloon and over to the Island which was another story.

'Can we go to the beach and have a swim in the sea?' asked Andrew.

'It's seven o'clock at night, you've had your bath, you are ready for bed and it's dark outside,' I said.

'Dad, I mean at the week-end.'

'Oh, sorry, I thought you meant right now. In that case I'll talk to your mum and see if we can organise a picnic for Saturday.'

'Wow! That's great dad. Thanks. Can I take a friend?'

'I'll have to check with mum but I think that will be OK.'

'It will be fine Dad,' said Andrew nodding his head in the direction of the kitchen where mum was chatting to Ah Moi. 'I'd like to take Paul from across the road. He said his dad wouldn't mind and he did invite me to his dad's sergeant's mess Christmas party last Christmas. He is my best pal dad.'

'Alright son, I'll talk to your mum who will talk to Paul's mum.' The conversation reminded me of an international conference; 'My people will talk to your people,' or words to that effect.

'Thanks dad.'

Saturday morning arrived and we were up early, had breakfast and on our way over the TWISK with the morning sun still rising and the sun roof of the car open. Andrew and Paul were sat in the back seats, reading or looking at the pictures of some children's books in between chatting to each other about what they were going to play at when they arrived at the beach. They each had a small rucksack containing their swimming costumes, goggles, spare dry costume, plimsolls to wear whilst swimming, a cold drink and some nibbles to munch on. The towels buckets, spades and other requirements for the beach, we had packed into the car. Some songs were sung as if we were setting off on holiday and down and around the twisting bends of the road we went.

We purchased tickets and joined the small queue for the car ferry, drove on and parked the car. We went upstairs to watch the Chinese sampans and junks with young children hanging over the sides performing their toiletries, or feeding the fish as it was politely referred to, as they sailed nonchalantly around huge American aircraft carriers and battleships still bringing their troops to Hong Kong from Vietnam for R&R (rest and recuperation). On reaching the Island we followed the cars off the ferry and down into the usual manic thoroughfare of Hong Kong; lorries, cars, yellow taxis, rickshaws, bicycles and people walking in all directions, carrying baskets full of wares, piglets under their arms, fish swimming in bags of water and chickens trussed up and carried upside down, but we knew our way through the streets and the road around the coast to the beach at Repulse Bay. It was only a matter of patience, great care and not being distracted by the peeping of horns, the ringing of bells and people stepping off the pavements to cross the road regardless of what was approaching.

The beach was busy but we found a space not too far from the car and quite near to the sea where we could both keep our eyes on the boys in the water. We settled down for an enjoyable afternoon in the warm sunshine as the lads made a large sand castle surrounded by a moat with buckets of water carried up from the sea. After a while, I took them into the water for a swim and a splash around while Carmine closed her eyes and relaxed. We had just finished some sandwiches and drinks; Andrew and Paul had ran back to the water when off to our left and down at the water's edge a group of children seemed to be terribly upset, shouting, crying and pointing into the water. As their parents started running towards them, Carmine looked up to check that the boys were alright paddling and called them back to her.

'I think you had better go and see what's wrong,' she said.

'I'll be right back,' I replied as I ran over with others to see what the commotion was all about.

There close to the edge were a large number of huge jelly fish. Quite a few of the children had been stung and were crying; a red rash was forming on their chests, arms and legs. 'I suggest,' said one man stepping out of the crowd 'that the parents take the children for treatment immediately up to the nearest doctor's surgery which is adjacent to the car park and that everyone stops going into the water for the rest of the afternoon. If anyone needs help, I'm sure there are folks here who will be willing to assist.'

There was a loud response of 'thank-you,' in English and Cantonese as children were gathered up by their parents. I related the story to Carmine and with the boys, we walked over to see the masses of pink and white jelly fish which looked like large, moving, mushroom domes, camouflaged in the water which is why the children hadn't seen them drifting in to the shallows where they were playing. Although they looked harmless, their sting was frightening and sore. It was a lesson for the boys to see what they looked like and to know that they must never to go anywhere near them. It was now early afternoon but we decided as the boys couldn't play in the water that we would pack everything up and drive round to Stanley Market which was only a few miles away.

The market was busy but once they each had a small packet of Chinese soft fruit sweets, the boys began to put the disappointment of leaving the beach early behind them. We met some army acquaintances and swapped the news from the New Territories, Kowloon and the Island. We let the lads choose a toy each from a stall which turned out to be major decisions but in the end they were happy with their choice. Carmine chose some new sunglasses and body cream from one stall whilst I selected a pair of flip flops and a white floppy hat from another. I glanced at my watch and realised that it was time to head back to the Ferry. Back at the car which was hot inside with the sun beating down on it, I opened the doors to let the air in whilst we used our sweat towels to wipe our brows and have a drink of orange juice from the portable ice box. When everyone was ready and finally comfortable, we jumped into the car and were on our way back to the ferry.

As we again crossed to the mainland, the boys were enthralled with the huge aircraft carrier sitting in the middle or the harbour and the circling helicopters ferrying men back and forwards to the Island. The sunshine on the water, the warmth of the afternoon, the rhythmic sound of the engines and the ferry creating bow waves as she ploughed over the sea taking us home, created a wonderful atmosphere of calm and tranquility. Carmine slipped her arm through mine and snuggled in close. 'I think that we could live here forever,' I said.

'Yes,' she replied, 'but I was just thinking about next spring when we will be going home. Perhaps we shouldn't think about that yet.'

'Maybe the army will extend my posting for another ten years,' I said. We looked at each other and laughed.

'Perhaps sometime in the future, we will be able to return.' I said not knowing that one day thirty three years later, our daughter Jackie who was then an air hostess with British Airways would come up from Edinburgh to our home in Callander and ask what we had planned for the week-end.

'Nothing special,' I would reply.

'Dad have you remembered it's your 40th Wedding Anniversary. Where are you planning to take mum?'

'I have bought a card, a nice one.'

'Tch!! That's the car in the drive, mums home. I have something to say but I'll wait until mum comes in.'

'Is everything alright Jackie?' I asked rather worried.

'Fine dad, just relax.'

'Hello Jackie, what a nice surprise. We weren't expecting you. How were the roads from Edinburgh? Busy?'

'Not too bad mum but come and sit down. I've put the kettle on but I have something to ask you and dad first and then we can all have a cup of tea. Now if you are both sitting comfortably, I'll begin.'

'Well, I'm flying out at the week-end for a few days to Hong Kong and as it is your Ruby Anniversary, I thought that you might like to come with me; stay with the crew and myself in a hotel on the Island.'

There was a silence for a moment before I shouted 'Wow! Great.'

'Really,' said Carmine.

'Really,' she replied.

I know that your passports are up to date and if you can drag yourselves away from the housework and weeding the garden, I'll arrange through the system for you to accompany me to Hong Kong. You will find a few changes since you were last there in 1968. The airport has moved from Kai Tak right out to Lantau Island, the buildings are even more numerous and taller, oh, and there's a tunnel for traffic under the harbour; life is just as hectic and exciting as ever it was.'

'Jackie that's great, your mum and I accept and I'll start packing to-night.'

'There is only one thing that I have to tell you,' said Jackie with a smile on her face. 'If the flight Standard Passenger and the Business Class seats are fully booked you might have to travel First Class.' Carmine and I looked at each other. 'We accept,' we shouted and with a First Class return ticket, we flew to Hong Kong where we celebrated our 40th Ruby Wedding Anniversary with Jackie, the Captain and all the crew of the BA Flight.

Jackie had to fly the next day with the crew to

Singapore on a duty twenty four hour trip whilst Carmine and I were left to enjoy Hong Kong. I remember her telling us that the following night when she returned to the hotel, she had knocked quietly on our room door and when there was no answer, she assumed that we had resorted to an early night, and went off to bed without seeing the note that we had put under her room door. It was only the following morning at breakfast that she discovered that we had been dancing the night away upstairs in the lounge bar until 2am; she couldn't believe it.

Two days later after touring the Island and taking the train up to visit Sui Pak Villa and the New Territories, we flew home and the Captain and the crew shook our hands and said farewell to us as we left the plane. What a wonderful Anniversary it turned out to be and happy memories in Hong Kong with Jackie.

Of course this was all in the future and at present we were on our way to Sek Kong. It was a pleasant drive and not too long before we were rolling down the hill into the village and home.

As we reached the drive, Paul's mum came across to thank us for taking him out and I picked up a note lying on the mat inside the front door. 'Would you like a cold drink Carmine?' I asked as she waved Paul and his mum off and came into the house.

'Oh please, I think we should put our feet up to-night and relax,' she said as she opened the fridge. Are you having a San Miguel or a Tiger beer Howard, and who is the note from?'

'Mick and Irene have invited us over for a barbecue to-night. All the gang are going to be there, the children are taking their pyjamas to change into and if they get tired they can pile into the spare room. If they don't hear to the contrary, they will see us around six thirty or when we are ready. Don't bring any food or drink as they have plenty in stock.'

'What do you think?' asked Carmine.

'Andrew,' I shouted, 'you are having an early bath, we are eating out to-night.'

'Good decision,' said Carmine.

Chapter 20 - Fanling Furniture

It was a long hot but enjoyable summer and at weekends, we travelled around the Colony visiting sites, places of interest, eating Chinese meals out, barbecues with friends and generally having fun and enjoying a good life. Andrew loved school, playing with his pals in the warm sunshine and swimming at the village pool.

One Sunday after lunch we went to look around the Fanling furniture factory where they had everything from coffee tables of every width and length with reversible tops, camphor wood chests of various sizes to lamp standards and numerous other items of furniture; all hand carved with Chinese patterns of choice. We were welcomed by the manager who introduced himself as Mr. Woo and offered a small glass of rice wine which was very pleasant. When asked which country we were from, he smiled and said that he thought the Scottish people were very friendly and 'nice'; probably everyone regardless of their nationality received the same treatment but it was a good welcome. He called over one of the workers from a nearby bench and asked him in Cantonese to show us around the factory. Chang speaks good English and will be delighted to answer any questions that you have and I will see you again before you leave.

Thank-you very much, I said as he bowed his head before retiring into his office.

All the workers were sitting on stools at low benches chipping and carving away at pieces of furniture with an array of chisels, wooden mallets and oddly shaped saws accompanied to a background of Chinese music.

There are many patterns to choose from said Chang and you can have all items the same which is normal or each can have a different pattern.'

'What are the costs?' Carmine asked.

It depends on the measurements, how many and the pattern you choose.

As we walked round the floor space we were

impressed by the standard of work being meticulously carried out. Most of the workmen raised their heads to smile and wave or nod to us.

'How long does that item take to make with complete carvings?' I asked, pointing to a large chest.

'About six weeks from ordering,' was the reply.

'What days are you open?' I asked.

Every day and every night to about ten o'clock but we change over, like you call shifts.'

'You must be very busy,' I said.

'Lots of customers,' he replied.

'Well thank-you Chang,' I said, 'we'll see Mr Woo at the office.'

'Dorgie,' (thank-you) he replied as he bowed his head.

When he realised that we were ready to go, Mr Woo came out of the office; 'I hope you liked our goods,' he said.

'We do and what a lovely smell throughout the factory' answered Carmine.

'If you purchase a camphor wood chest the rich aroma will pass through your home every time you open the lid,' he said.

'What is the system of purchasing?' I asked.

'Please come into the office, have a seat,' he said gesturing towards some comfortable chairs placed around a circular table 'and I'll explain it to you. When you are ready to buy, call back to see me and tell me what you would like us to make for you and the pattern of your choice. At the moment there is a waiting list which is why I say about two months. Once I know what your choice of purchase is, I will give you the price and the time scale. When your order is being worked on, you can come here to the factory and watch your furniture being made and the patterns being carved into the wood; no machines, all done by hand. Once we have started carving, we cannot change the pattern and therefore we will require a small deposit before starting work. You mentioned that you were living in Sek Kong and I'm sure that you know a number of customers there who have purchased and will recommend our reliable work to you.'

'Yes, we do,'

'We can also package your order up and export it to the UK or we can deliver it to your home at Sek Kong. Please take a copy of the different patterns that we can carve for you.

'Well thank-you Mr Woo, we have plenty to think about but I can assure you that we will be back to order. Thank -you again.'

'Dorgie, thank you,' he said.

'As we climbed into the car, Carmine suggested that we pop round to see Sue and Arthur at Su Pak Villa. 'What a great idea,' I said and we did.

Although I saw Arthur every day at the Company Office of HQ.48 Brigade, it was good to be able to see him socially and both Carmine and I had never forgot how he and Sue had helped us settle into the way of life when we first arrived in Hong Kong. Tommy and Andrew went downstairs to play at the sand area of the garden while Sue plated up some sandwiches, cakes and prepared some soft drinks in spite of Carmine telling her not to bother.

'San Mig, or Tiger beer Howard?' asked Arthur.

Before I could ask who was driving home, Carmine shouted across the room, 'I'll drive,'

'Thank-you darling. San Miguel please Arthur,' who looked at Carmine, smiled, nodded and winked at me.

We had a lovely afternoon on Arthur's veranda and the conversation with laughs included, just rolled on throughout the afternoon.

'You two just never seem to get any older,' said Carmine looking at Sue and Arthur. 'Time rushes by but we must meet up again soon. Come and see us at Sek Kong.'

As we gathered Andrew up, we said our farewells. 'See you to-morrow at work Arthur.'

'You will indeed Howard.' the Brigadier will be sending for you but don't worry, it's good news.'

'Tell me,' I said. 'You know that I won't be able to sleep to-night.'

'See you to–morrow Howard,' Arthur shouted as he waved us off and Carmine put the car into first gear.

I didn't press for an Answer as I knew a confidential signal must have come through and Arthur couldn't divulge its contents.

'Bye,' we shouted as we drove through the gates at Su Pak Villa heading down the country road to Sek Kong.

The following morning, I was called into see the Brigadier who congratulated me on being promoted to Staff Sergeant Instructor. Somehow the word did get around and as per custom it cost me a few Hong Kong dollars over the bar that lunch time in the sergeant's mess. That evening, Carmine and I opened a celebration bottle of bubbly.

Chapter 21 - Tokyo

Two weeks after our initial visit to the furniture factory at Fanling, we went back to place our order which was a large camphor wood chest, a magazine rack, a long reversible coffee table/stool with a floral padded top, two matching small reversible tables, a fire screen and a large table lamp carved as a Chinese lady with a baby waiting for her husband to return safely home from the sea. All had a hand carved Chinese Willow Tree Pattern which we had chosen and the order would be delivered to our quarter at Sek Kong within a few weeks. 45 years later they still grace our home.

It had been a long hot but enjoyable summer with some families from the village going home to UK. or moving on to Singapore or even Germany with their regiments. New faces were appearing in the village.

I now had my flight details for Tokyo which was flying out on the 29th November with Japanese Airlines and flying back on the 22nd December 1967 in time for Christmas. During this period of time, I would be examined for my grading of 1st Dan black belt. The winter months were creeping in and fires were being lit in Sek Kong as I packed my case for Tokyo. I knew it would be very cold in Japan, and I made sure that I had warm casual clothing with two judo suits and my brown belt. The Gurkha driver who was taking me down to Kai Tak Airport, drove the land rover up to the front door of our army quarter and I placed my case in the back.

'Good luck,' said Carmine, 'just remember all the training that you have done and keep calm. Andrew and I will be thinking of you and it will be Christmas when you come home.'

With a tear in my eye, I hugged Andrew and kissed Carmine. I jumped into the land rover, waved cheerio and I was off to Kai Tak Airport. The flight was quite busy with Japanese travellers returning home and I fell asleep after the meal. As I left Customs and stepped into the huge main airport lounge, I eventually saw a driver holding up a card saying Mr. Gee. I felt relieved that having arrived safely, someone was here to meet me and drive me to the British Embassy. It was a large limousine and although the driver after putting my luggage in the boot, opened the passenger door for me, I said that I would rather sit in the front and talk to him if that was alright.

'Of course sir as you please. I gather from your accent that you are from the homeland sir and would be delighted to hear what part of Scotland you are from, all about Hong Kong and your purpose here in Tokyo unless of course, it is a secret mission.' We looked at each other and laughed.

'May I ask your name?'

'It's Callum MacDonald sir but usually I'm just called Mac.'

'Well Mac, please call me Howard and I was born and bred in Edinburgh. Where are you from?'

Isle of Lewis, sir, I mean Howard.'

'I'm here to try to gain my black belt at the Kodokan Mac.'

'You will know George Kerr from Edinburgh then?' It seemed everyone in Tokyo knew George Kerr.

'I haven't met him but know all about him and I will certainly look him up when I return to Edinburgh from Hong Kong.'

'Do you enjoy living in Hong Kong Howard?'

'Yes,' I replied and before I had finished telling him about the Colony and he had briefed me on Tokyo, we were driving through the large gates of the Embassy.

'I'll be waiting here for you Howard to take you to the Kodokan once you have seen Colonel Blair Smyth the Military Attaché.

I was meeting the Colonel for a briefing on the ways and the etiquette of the Japanese people and to receive my funding allowance for the trip. After shaking my hand and welcoming me to Japan, he asked if I had enjoyed a comfortable flight to which I replied that I had and thanked him for sending his driver to meet me. He gave me a telephone contact number should I have any difficulties and confirmed that the driver would be outside the Kodokan at 0930 hours to take me to the airport on the 22nd of December which would be plenty time for my return flight to Hong Kong.

'I wish you the very best of luck in gaining your black belt', he said. 'I will hear how you get on. Oh! and before I forget, you had better sign for these.' He lifted a bundle of notes from his desk; 48,000 Yen for your food, accommodation and any travelling expenses you may have.' He must have seen my eyes light up.

'It's not as much as you might think,' he said. 'It amounts to £300 and I will of course require receipts which you should keep and pass to your Paymaster when you get home to 48 Brigade. Spend it wisely, as food and purchases are very expensive in Japan. Keep out of mischief and no political incidents. Once again the very best of luck; my driver, Mr. Macdonald whom you have met will take you round now to the Kodokan at Bunkyo Ku.'

'Thank you very much for your help and my expenses sir, I've never held so much money in my hand since I last played monopoly.'

He laughed and shook my hand again as he showed me out of his office and pointed down the corridor in the direction of the car park to where his driver was waiting.

It did not take long to reach the Kodokan and after collecting my luggage, I shook hands with Mac who wished me good luck and confirmed that he would be here to meet me on the 22nd when he hoped that I would be in possession of a black judo belt.

'Konnichiwa, onamaewa onegai shimasu?' (Hello, what is your name please) asked the receptionist, repeating the words in English.

'Mr. Gee.' I replied and to my relief, the receptionist had my name on the sheets and was expecting me to arrive when I did.

'Ah!! Gee–san. Konnnichiwa ogenki desu ka,' (Good afternoon, how are you?') she said, bowing her head. As it must have been obvious that I didn't know what she meant; 'Good afternoon and how are you?' she explained with a smile. 'Are you looking forward to your stay with us? I believe that you have come from Scotland but are living in Hong Kong at present. You will know George Kerr a famous judoka from Edinburgh who has trained here for a long time before going home to become the Scottish and British Champion.

I smiled and wasn't sure which question to answer first but before I could say anything she handed me three keys on a ring, one to my room 202, one to the front door of the building and one to the small safe in my room. 'The front door of the building is closed at eleven o'clock at night when all training is finished,' she explained. She handed me a card for information about the opening and closing times of the centre and times of all meals which had to be paid for as purchased. To-morrow I will give you an account for the cost of your room for your stay which the manager would be grateful if you would pay in advance, like a good Scots person,' she said as she smiled.

'There is a telephone number on the card; if you have any difficulties in the city, just ring here and we will help you,'

'Thank-you very much,' I said.

'You will be training,' she continued, 'in the International Dojo under various Senseis who will give you the times that they will be available in the dojo for coaching; they will expect you to be there but of course you are free to enter the main Training Dojo whenever you wish but be careful to learn the etiquette required. Also be aware that when you step on to the tatami, all the young students of black belt grades will want to test your skill in randori. I hope you are very fit Gee-san; you must avoid injury and be ready for your grading examination, the details of which will be given to you within the next few days.'

'Domo arigatoo gazimas,' (thank you very much) Gee-san,' she said pointing to the lift and again bowing to me. I thanked her and just before I stepped into the lift, she called 'Oh, Sumimasen. (Excuse me) Inokuma-san sends his regards and says that he will see you soon and he will attend your grading. He has many students and fans and you are very honoured to be remembered by him.' Although the reception area was by now quite busy, everyone stopped talking, looked at me and started clapping; it seemed that just to be known by Isao Inokuma was enough for me to be respected. I was rather embarrassed but smiled, gave a bow, stepped into the lift and pressed the number 2 button.

As I stepped out of the lift room 202 was just to the left down the corridor and I turned the key in the lock. The room was small but looked comfortable and was spotlessly clean. I put my case on to a stool by the bed and pulled the curtains back to look out over Central Tokyo. I opened the small fridge but it was empty and realised that I had obviously to fill it myself with food and soft drinks once I had been to the shops. There was a small safe and my third key fitted it perfectly. I was intending to hang my coat, clothes and judo suits up in the wardrobe, have a quick shower get my bearings and find some shops when there was a knock on the door. I opened it to find a tall, about six feet, fair haired lad who smiled and said, 'Hi, I'm booked in to room 194, a few doors further down the corridor, and my name is Ken Foster,' he said with a slight drawl 'and I'm not an American before you ask, I'm a Canadian and I've been practising judo for about three years.'

'Hi Ken, good to meet you,' I said holding out my hand to shake his. 'I'm Howard and I have just arrived. Do you live in Canada?'

'I do live in and have travelled from Canada. I arrived 3 days ago and reception asked me to meet you and help you to get to know the systems for meals etc. Like you, I'm a brown belt going for my Ist Dan in the same examination as you and I wondered if we could practice our katas together for the grading if that is alright with you. I'm going down town shortly to buy some shopping if you would like to come.'

'Yes that would be great Ken; if you could give me thirty minutes to finish unpacking and have a quick shower and change.'

'Yep of course Howard, you give my door a rap when you are ready and we can talk all the way into town.'

We decided to share a taxi and within minutes we were in the heart of bustling Tokyo. The shops had large windows and were already decorated with festive goods and all sorts of lights and mechanical movable toys and clothes on the waxwork dummies. Although Japan is largely Buddhist or of the Shinto religion, the spirit of Christmas was everywhere or at least the commercial aspect was.

'I suggest that we have something to eat and have a chat Howard. Do you like seafood?'

'A good idea and I love seafood.'

The Sushi bar was quite busy but we found a couple of tall stools at a large circular counter with a slow revolving conveyor belt in front of it where varieties of sea foods on plates could be selected and picked up with bowls of rice or noodles as they continually passed in front of us. A system of replenishment on the belt was operated by waiters wearing white shirts, bow ties and side hats worn at a jaunty angle. Selection was helped by coloured photographs and descriptions of the individual meals which could be studied on the counter prior to making a decision of choice.

'What is the method of payment for the dishes Ken?'

When we have finished eating, our choice of food per plate is totalled up by the waiters who give us a slip which we take to the cashier over there at the till,' he said pointing to a lady sitting at a desk en route to the door. 'Are you happy to share the costs and are you organised with your yen?'

'I am on both accounts and also starving.'

'Me too,' said Ken. 'Can you use the chopsticks?'

'Living in Hong Kong, I sure can. Let's get started.'

As we ate, Ken briefed me on the rules and customs of the Kodokan that he had picked up these last few days. 'The usual etiquette upon stepping on to the mats prevail Howard but be aware that one also bows when you enter the dojo. Bowing is the mark of respect for others especially the Senseis and senior grades on the mat. All bows are carried out in a formal manner, not just a nod of the head and that goes when starting randori with an opponent. When the large drum which is supported on a wooden frame is beat it means a very senior Sensei, possibly 8th or 9th Dan has stepped on to the mats. Everyone must stop and bow to him or even sometimes kneel and bow as dictated by the senior instructor already on the mats. The sounding of a gong may also mean the end of training for example for lunch or the start of a formal training session.'

'Around the edges of the tatami are the warm up areas but as soon as you step across the red markings you are entering the randori or contest area and you will be challenged immediately by the young black belts wanting to try out their latest techniques and skills; they will decide individually when to move on to another opponent and allow a waiting, eager contestant to challenge you. They love to see how good we Europeans are and if they put a choke or arm lock on, make sure you submit immediately because you won't escape from it, oh and neither size nor weight matters in randori. If you need to leave the mats for the toilet, adjust any strapping or just need to take a breather, get out of the contest area quick before you are challenged again.'

I nodded to show that I understood. 'We will be expected to report to the Overseas Student's Dojo tomorrow morning with the other International Students and be warmed up ready for the Sensei's coaching. Don't expect any tuition as such but he will watch you training and practicing and say a few words or demonstrate how your throwing techniques can be improved; all to be taken very seriously; no messing around. If you get a bump or a knock, you will be expected to leave the mats and go and sort yourself out; there is first aid available with some help from an attendant in the small room at the back of the dojo but we are expected to provide our own strapping and supports for ankles, knees and elbows not to mention heat cream or liniment.'

'Which students are at present in the International Dojo?' I asked.

'Three or four Americans; don't mistake them for Canadians, a couple of Germans, some Dutch, a number of French, some Scandinavians and a few from Russia and other European countries. Their grades range from 1st Kyu brown belts to 3rd and 4th Dan grades black belts. They don't all stay in the Kodokan as some work in central Tokyo and some live with various Japanese families but we will meet the others from the Kodokan throughout the day and at meals. Have a good breakfast and we can eat in the Kodokan Restaurant for lunch but

151

it is mainly Japanese food. There are tables set aside for self-catering and it is a good idea to make up some rolls at breakfast which we can eat in that part of the restaurant. Normally the day will end between 4 and 5 pm if your body can last that long. Of course you may not feel like eating after being thrown so often, at least until you find your strength, mobility and skill to stay on your feet and start dominating your opponent. We can return in the evening to see the top judoka contest training when we can learn a lot just relaxing and watching.'

'Sounds a really good idea,' I said. 'That does appeal to me.'

'We will have to practice our Katas (Demonstrations of formal judo techniques including throws, groundwork, arm locks and choke locks) as well as answer theory questions on the history of judo and of course the examination will finish with contests between competitors of grades decided by the examiners but generally as I understand it between brown and black belts of 1st and 2nd Dan grades. Some Japanese students will almost certainly be selected.'

'Do you know that all universities in Japan have a Judo club of around 60 members who have home and away matches against each other like football or rugby teams back home. They don't require a colour grading system from white through to brown as we do; their students start at white and when ready are examined and awarded their 1st Dan black belt.

'I didn't know that and I am very impressed. It looks like we will be working very hard over the next few weeks. My own instructor back in Hong Kong, Takeo Iwami warned me that the instructors here are watching us at all times and will report on our skills, technique, efforts and attitude which will be taken into account at our grading.'

'Wait until you see the number of dojos, the size of the main dojo and the number of judoka training at any one time,' said Ken. 'I'm told that there is nowhere else in the world like it and I believe it.'

'Thanks for briefing me. I can't wait to get started to-morrow morning.'

'How do you feel about us working together Howard?'

'Well now that I'm beginning to understand what you're saying, I'd be delighted to practice with you. I think that we will make a good team and with a bit of luck we'll both gain our black belts.' We laughed and shook hands. 'Thanks for your help Ken I do appreciate it. I think now I'd quite like to pick up some bits and pieces before heading back.'

'Right I'll leave you here Howard as I want to go down to the post office. You can either go back by taxi or jump on a bus from the stop across the road; they all pass the Kodokan and I'll see you at breakfast around 8am to-morrow.'

'See you in the morning then,' and we went our separate ways. I thought that I might have a quick look into the main dojo before retiring for an early night. It was an important day that lay ahead.

I had another shower, laid out my kit for the morning and set my alarm for 0630 hours, jumped into bed and fell asleep.

Chapter 22 - Judo Training

When the alarm went off, I realised that I had spent my first night in Japan and was now very apprehensive about my first day of training.

'Ohayoo gozaimasu (Good morning) Gee- san,' the receptionist called as I passed the desk on my way to the restaurant for breakfast. 'Did you sleep well?'

'Ohayoo gozaimasu,' I replied bowing as if I was an old hand at communicating with the Japanese language and customs. 'Yes, I slept very well thank-you.' It was a relief that the house rules allowed us to dress casual for meals; I wore a polo shirt and tracksuit bottoms.

I ate a light breakfast before returning to my room where I had a quick wash, cleaned my teeth, made my bed and generally tidied up before changing into my judo suit which I wore under my tracksuit. I had as always slept with my window open and decided to leave it open a little at the top to keep the air circulating. I locked my valuables in the safe and realised that I still had thirty minutes before knocking on Ken's door on my way to the lift. I sat on the chair gazing out of the window thinking of home, did some deep breathing exercises, picked up my holdall containing my brown belt, a towel, a couple of soft drinks, knee and elbow supports, some bandages and elastoplasts , some money for lunch, bits and pieces and my flip flops. I had decided to wear trainers around the centre and only put my flip flops on in the dojo area ensuring that I didn't trip on the stairs or on the ornate mats around the reception. I locked my room door and made my way down to room 192 where Ken was ready and waiting for me.

As the dojos were straight through from the main reception area, the wearing of judo suits underneath tracksuits when moving around the centre and for going into the restaurant for meals was allowed. Judoka living outside the Kodokan would normally change into and out of their judo suits in the changing rooms and shower before leaving the building to go home.

As we went through the swing doors the atmosphere changed to a sense of decorum mingling with the sounds of intense activity. The first dojo on the right had 'Kendo' in bold letters above the door and when I entered, I saw participants in pairs dressed in black baggy trousers with a shiny matching breast plate, protective face guards stretching over the back of their heads and heavy gloves wielding large bamboo swords. They were moving up and down the mats attacking each other to score by hitting their opponent on the target area. They wore no shoes and the whole scene was reminiscent of the days of the Samurai Warriors from where I understood the sport derived from

The doors opposite read above it Aikido and inside participants were dressed similar to the Kendo participants without the bamboo swords, masks, breast plates and gloves. Again it was bare feet on the tatami. Aikido was a form of self-defense which was introduced by the monks and holy men travelling throughout the land when after the Samurai era, the carrying of weapons unless authorised by the government was banned. Monks and travellers were easy prey to bandits and they devised a form of self-defense which didn't require weapons. All movements were quick but defensive by use of the hands and feet and involved pulling or drawing an attacker off balance by using his weight and his momentum to upset the rhythm of his balance in various directions; twisting wrists and bending fingers leaving him vulnerable to arm breaks, hand chops or use of the heel of the foot to various vulnerable parts of the body. Once perfected, the actions could be lethal but were within the laws of Japan. I was fascinated and tempted to stay and watch but Ken reminded me that we mustn't be late for our Sensei. I didn't know then but some years later, I would be involved with the introduction of minimum force arresting techniques that our soldiers would use throughout the troubled areas of the world; based on the art of Aikido.

Left and right of the corridor were smaller dojos where students appeared to be limbering and loosening up, bending and stretching, practising groundwork, perhaps just recovering from the injuries of strains and pulled muscles. Ahead, next to the International Student's Dojo were the changing rooms, toilets and showers and I made a mental note of not having to go too far if the call of nature kicked in. Two large double swing doors dominated the bottom of the corridor leading into the Main Training Dojo but tucked away in the right hand corner of the corridor was a door that I couldn't resist opening. The smell nearly knocked me off my feet. Looking upwards, just below the ceiling, I could see long poles stretching horizontally across the large room with hundreds of judo suits on coat hangers dangling from the poles; heat seemed to be rising from the hot radiators to mingle with the damp, sweaty judo suits creating a grizzly scene of limp bodies hanging in a room of rising steam.

'What's going on here Ken?' I asked.

'Well,' he started to explain; 'after training is finished the students can wash and rinse their sweaty judogi out and hang them up to dry or just hang them up to air instead of carrying them back and forwards from home.'

'How do they get them up there and retrieve them?'

'With these long poles with hooks on the end,' said Ken pointing to the corner where the poles were standing, ready for use.

'How do they know which is their suits?'

'A good question,' he said. 'I don't think they worry too much as long as they have a suit that they can train in. Of course they also require one that roughly fits. They seem to be very honest, probably very dishonourable not to return it. I think that various groups hang them up together which might help a bit to identify their own. They do keep hold of their own individual belts.'

'Amazing,' I thought to myself.

'Better we take our suits back to our room,' suggested Ken.

'Definitely,' I agreed.

'Right,' said Ken 'we better get in to the dojo and warm up before the Sensei arrives.'

There was only an American and a German

student in before us and after introductions, shaking of hands and some small talk we started warming and loosening up. Gradually other students arrived and by the time the Sensei arrived we were all doing uchi komi (working in pairs going through the motions of throws, gripping, holding, turning, twisting and pulling without carrying out the actual throws) which saved time waiting for your partner to get up off the tatami.

When the Sensei came on to the mat, we stopped our training, turned towards him and bowed; he returned the bow and signaled for us to continue. Throughout the morning, we worked hard and continuous with the Sensei watching and correcting our head position when committing to throws, the turning of our hips, our footwork in attack and defense, hand grips, strong arms, flexibility in movement and awareness of our opponent's intentions.

When we finally stopped for lunch, Sensei Otani called us into a semi-circle to address us. He looked every inch as someone not to meddle with. He looked about five foot eight inches tall, very broad in the shoulders with a strong jaw line held up by two massive cauliflower ears. His straight back and carriage around the mats portrayed a man of confidence within his trade. He told us that he was a 6th Dan, welcomed us to the International Student's Dojo and said that although we had worked well, we had not worked hard enough and if we hoped to pass our examination he would expect to see a big improvement in our work rate and performance after the lunch break.

He informed us that our Grading examination would start at 10 O'clock on 17th December; Katas and demonstration of techniques would be first followed by contests. If successful, the presentation of black belts would be shortly after the contests had finished and the judges had discussed their decisions. 'I hope you all understand the importance of this date; please do not fly home before arrangements are complete,' he emphasised. We looked at each other and smiled.

'Inokuma-san, the Olympic Gold Medallist and a number of Senior Sensei will be in the dojo on the 17th and will also attend the presentation should any of you pass'. A cold shiver ran up my spine. 'Go and have lunch now and be back for 1:30 pm. May I suggest that you have very light lunch.' We gave a kneeling bow to Sensei Otani and waited until he had stepped off the tatami before we followed him.

'How are you feeling Ken?' I said as we sat down in the dining room.

'Not too bad but I have a feeling that after lunch we are going to be tested on our body strengths, physical ability, stamina and skills,' he replied.

'Well I'm just going to have a ham sandwich and a soft drink. What are you having?'

'Same as you.'

After stretching our legs in the small garden and a quick chat with the other students, we all headed back to the dojo and by the time the Sensei had arrived we had warmed up with exercises and uchi komi.

'We are going into the Main Dojo where you can watch for fifteen minutes before you will be challenged by some of the students when you must try your very best at randori. Do you all understand?' The deathly hush answered the question for everyone.

As we moved next door, the atmosphere changed immediately. The Dojo was huge and the contest area was filled with moving judoka striving to throw opponents on to their backs for a full ippon (point) which would win any contest. After a few minutes, I think he forgot the 15 min scenario, he announced that we should now step on to the contest area.

3rd and 4th Dan grades, appeared from all over the tatami and with a bow took hold of us and pulled us into the middle of the contest area where there was no escape and before we knew it, we were being thrown by every spectacular throw in their curriculum; Harai Goshi (Hip sweep), Okuri Ashi Barai (Foot sweep) Uchimata [Inner thigh throw), Hane Goshi (Hip spring) followed by throw after throw. Then it seemed the turn of young 1st and 2nd Dans, and by now we were struggling to stay on our feet, get our breath back and think of how to counter and even attack these formidable opponents. When the gong went for the end of the afternoon session, I let out a sigh of relief and Ken's words were not repeatable in the decorum of the dojo. All the international students felt the same although some had experienced randori in the Main Dojo before and had known what to expect. The only thing that I had perfected was my break fall.

'See you all in our own dojo to-morrow at 10am,' said Otani- san. 'Sore dewa mate, sayoonara' (See you later, good bye) We were lucky that Chuck, an American student could translate for us.

After showering and lying down on top of the bed for about an hour, I rapped Ken's door, woke him up and we went downstairs for our evening meal and a chat with some of the other lads in the class.

'Do you fancy dancing tonight?' asked Ken.

'My knees couldn't take it. I'll be lucky if I can climb into bed tonight,' I replied. 'It's an early night for me.'

'Me too,' agreed Ken. 'Only joking,'

As we stepped out of the lift, Ken shouted that he would see me in the morning.

'Ok,' I shouted, 'I'll knock on your door for breakfast.'

'I rubbed my aching limbs with liniment, and jumped into bed. I left the curtains opened to enjoy the lights of downtown Tokyo and fell asleep.'

Chapter 23 - Black Belt Grading

Over the next few days, we all worked hard and every afternoon when we entered the Main Dojo, we were thrown on to our backs and when the gong went, we crawled back to our rooms to shower, rub liniment into our aching muscles and joints, then lay down on top of our beds. But gradually we started holding our own and were beginning to challenge and get the better of our opponents which did more for our aching bodies than the liniment and balm.

We were now working very hard and on some evenings we were actually going back on to the mats in our own dojo to practice techniques. This meant that we could concentrate during the day on the randori; learning from the 3rd and 4th Dans with a combination of challenging them or even just watching their skills when they challenged each other or were challenged by even higher grades.

Chuck and Marty both Americans, Gunthar a German, Daniel from Holland and French Pierre who all lived in the Kodokan, joined Ken and I most nights for a beer in the small beer house just outside the Kodokan after training, and then the evening meal. We all had a few knocks and visible bruises but we were staying clear of injuries as best as we could which might prevent us taking our grading exam.

'We need a break,' said Chuck one evening while we were enjoying a beer.

'Any suggestions?' asked Pierre

'Why don't we take the train down to Osaka, it's not too long a journey.'

'It will certainly give us a welcomed break,' I said.

'Mein muscles vill be grateful,' said Gunthar with a stern face, unconsciously rubbing his shoulder.

'Right we're all agreed then,' shouted Chuck. 'Roll on Sunday.'

Sunday morning arrived and we all shared two taxis down to the station and as there wasn't a train that morning to Osaka we caught the early train to Shimizu on the coast, south of Yokohama. We sat back and relaxed at the tables and the conversation never stopped until Ken looked out the window and shouted, 'Wow!, look at that.'

We all moved across to the window to see the snowcapped Mount Fuji in all its glory rising behind Lake Kawaguchi. It was simply a magnificent sight and we all stared out of the window until the train carried us out of view.

We had a lovely peaceful day by the sea and the fresh breezes filled up our lungs, reinvigorating our bodies, clearing our heads and replenishing our will to succeed in our quest to gain a black belt. Watching the Japanese way of life as it passed us by was relaxing and after a few beers, more sushi, a good laugh and the train back to Tokyo, we were ready to face Monday morning.

The days rolled by and on the day before the grading, we did no randori but practised our Katas, and all techniques including groundwork, arm locks and choke locks as we knew that we would be asked to demonstrate from each category. After laying out my clean judogi and all my supports for my ankles, knees and elbows, I had an early night but it was sometime before I fell asleep after which it seemed only minutes before the alarm went off.

On the morning of the Grading, I was down early for a light breakfast and by 0930 hours we were all on the tatami of the Main Dojo, warmed up and awaiting the arrival of the examiners. Sensei Otani arrived first and told us all to relax. 'Remember how hard you have trained,' he said, 'be confident and do your very best,' We waited, tried to relax and watched the clock.

Sensei Isao Inokuma arrived, removed his shoes, stepped on to the tatami and bowed. Sensei Otani introduced him to everyone. He wished us all good luck and made a point of shaking my hand as if we were old friends. He bowed and stepped off the mat, taking a seat in the front row of the spectator's seats. Sensei Otani then introduced the two Examiners; 7th Dan T.Daigo and 9th Dan S. Kotanio

'Did he say 9th Dan?' asked Ken.
'He did,' I answered.

'Dat is very gut,' said Gunthar.

The competition area was divided into two and Sensei Otani read out the two groups to perform in each area. Everyone was to fight each other in their group. The winner and runner up of Area1 would cross over on to Area 2 to meet the winner and runner up on that mat. The other contestants would be divided into a further two groups who would compete against each other. Referees and judges had been appointed and took up their positions with the referees in the centre and the judges on chairs at opposite corners.

I was determined to win and when I drew an American in my first contest, I pulled him around, didn't let him settle and turned him over for a full point with 'Ippon seoi nage'.

My next contest was with Gunthar who was very strong and resisted my efforts to tip him off balance; I feinted with Tai Otoshi (Body drop) and caught him with Kouchi Gari (Small inside clip) and knocked him to the ground where I pinned him down as the referee called 'Osaekomi' and held him for 30 seconds, a full ippon.

Next up was another very fast moving American called Wilber and I decided to pull tight with my right hand on his left lapel, pulling his left shoulder down whilst my left hand was tugging at his right sleeve. I turned my hips fully and swept his right leg away with Harai goshi for a wazari (half point) and when he landed on the mat, I placed an arm lock on for a submission. At this stage the winner who was Ken and the runner up a Russian in Area1 crossed over on to our mat and my next opponent was the Russian. He was breathing heavy and I decided not to waste time trying different moves. We bowed when the referee called 'rei' and on 'hajime' I took my grip, feinted turning right with my hips, changed to left and threw him on to his back with a right sided Harai goshi (hip sweep)

Ken won his contest and we now faced each other. Having trained together, we knew each other's strengths and weaknesses and it was always going to be a close match.

'Hajime,' called the referee. We bowed and took hold of each other's judogi pulling tight and trying to get our favourite grips. As we moved around I tried Uchi Mata (inner thigh sweep] but Ken resisted and I resisted his counter attempt at Hane Goshi (inner leg lift). I feinted Uchi Mata ,and swept his outer ankle in Kosoto Gari (small outside clip) knocking him down to the ground and before he could gather his wits I transferred my left hand on to his right collar with the fingers of my right hand inside his left collar, ducked my head underneath both hands and had him in a tight choke lock which he resisted but I wasn't letting go and as I increased the pressure, he had to either submit by tapping me twice or pass out. He submitted.

I thought that would be the end of the contests but suddenly two young Japanese black belts appeared on our contest area. Ken had a narrow victory against the first. I was tiring a bit now, 'but I had to go for it.' The second one stepped forward, we bowed and as the referee shouted 'Hajime' we tried to take hold of our favourite grips. We attempted throws, feinted and attempted throws and counter throws. We pulled and pushed, stepped off the contest area and were brought back on again by the referee. Both of us almost scored but the other twisted out of the attacker's movements and tried to counter throw but the momentum took us both off the mat. After 3 minutes, the bell went and we both collapsed on to our knees before standing up, adjusting our belts around our judogi awaiting the judge's decision. There would be no draw given. When called the judge's had to raise their flag and point to the winner. If the decision was one each, the referee would decide. Both judges pointed to me; I had won on aggression. I was absolutely thrilled but realised that I still had one contest to go. Ken, again won his final contest against the other Japanese student with a wazari (half point)

I had a few minutes break before being called back on to the mat. As far as I could tell my friends were having mixed fortunes in their contests and it might be touch and go who would be successful in gaining their black belt.

'Last bout,' I heard the announcer call in English followed by my name and the name of the other

Japanese competitor whom I'm sure had been thrown in to test us to the limit. I knew that he had been warming up but was fresh for the contest; it was a test for me but I had to concentrate.

Hajime called the referee and the clock started ticking its last three minutes. We moved around the tatami weighing each other up before taking a hold and he immediately swept both my feet off the ground on to my knees for a 'Koka' (knockdown) 3 points but I was up, feinted to grab his collar but transferred both my hands down on to his trousers at knee level, lifted him up as I swept my right leg behind both his legs and knocked him down. He twisted on to his side for a Wazari (half point) and I followed him down on to the ground with my weight on top of his chest; my right arm was around his neck and gripping his collar and I tucked his right arm under my left arm with my hand holding his sleeve as though in a vice. 'Osaekomi' (holding) called the referee, pointing with the palm of his hand towards us on the ground and the timekeeper immediately started the clock ticking towards the 25 seconds required to gain my other half point. My head was low down the side of his head and although he twisted ,struggled and tried to escape my hold there was no way that he was going to escape and he didn't; the bell went for time. I had won all my contests but decisions were still to be made by the examiners. Ken and I shook hands and said 'well done' to each other. It was a great moment for both of us.

After a short break, we were called into our pairs in preparation for the demonstration of Katas, (formal movements and throws), groundwork (ne-waza), holding and escapes (osae waza), arm locks (kansetsu-waza) and choke locks (shime-waza).

The preparation time that Ken and I had spent, paid off and although every movement wasn't perfect, we knew and carried out all our demonstrations as asked of us whilst others were struggling to remember them nor hadn't practiced various techniques to the standard required.

The gong went which heralded the end of the examination and while we, the students bowed and left the dojo for the changing rooms to wash, cool down and have some refreshing soft drinks, the examiners retired to a room adjacent to the Dojo to discuss the results. It was about 30 minutes before we were called back into the Dojo where we were asked to form a semi-circle to hear the results.

Sensei Otani stepped forward with a millboard in his hand and explained that six students had failed to reach the standard of the 1st Dan black belt grade but all would be given a second opportunity in two weeks' time and should make accommodation and suitable training arrangements. Everyone was now looking at each other nervously. He then proceeded to read out the names of the unfortunate few of which there was 1 American, 1 French, 2 Scandinavians, 1 Russian and 1 Romanian. Although we were sorry for them, a sigh of relief went around the rest of the group. We all offered them our condolences and our best wishes to them in their next examination.

As our names were called, we stepped forward to receive our black belts from 9th Dan Sensei Kotani and to be congratulated and have our hands shaken by 7th Dan Daigo and Olympic Gold Medallist Isao Inokuma, who spoke to me and said that it had been a pleasure to meet me; I replied that it had been an honour to meet him again and I thanked him for keeping his promise and making time to come to the grading to-day. We both smiled, shook hands again and I felt so proud being congratulated by a living legend from the world of judo.

All the students said a special thanks to Sensei Otani for guiding us through our grading and presented to him a small gift that we had all chipped in to buy. We bowed in respect as he left the Dojo.

Most of us ordered a second black belt from the shop in the Kodokan and requested that various wording of choice be sewn on to both belts. I had 'Howard' sewn in gold Japanese lettering on one end of both belts and 'Scotland' on the other and although they have been well used, the lettering is still there to this day. That night, those who didn't pass were invited to join us but opted for a quiet reflective night whilst the rest of us celebrated with a meal at a local restaurant and washed it down with quite a few beers. There was no rush to get up the following morning but I wanted to double check that my flight details were all in order which they were and I telephoned the Embassy to ensure that a car had been arranged as previously agreed. The next few days Ken and I wandered around the shops in Tokyo buying Christmas presents. He was going home to Canada and his flight home was the day before mine. I was sad to see him go but as we shook hands, he promised he would write once he had settled down.

I just wanted to get home now and when Mac turned up at the front door of the Kodokan to drive me to the airport, I didn't tell him that I had been ready and waiting for two hours. He insisted on seeing my black belt, shook my hand and said 'Well done; I'll tell the boss,'

Inside my pocket was the confirmation letter of having passed my grading which I would send off to the secretary of the Army Judo Association in Aldershot who would register my grade with the British Judo Association in London.

I slept on the plane but was awake long before it touched down at Kaitak. A Gurkha driver was waiting for me with my transport to Sek Kong and once again I was so happy to be home that a tear rolled down my cheek as Andrew and Carmine ran out the front door to meet me.

Training with Isao Inokuma

Isao Inokuma
Gold Medal winner
1964 Olympics

168

Chapter 24 - Farewell to Hong Kong

Christmas was upon us, the coal fires were burning bright throughout the village and our homes were warm and cosy. It was not cold in comparison to the UK but after the tropical summer, an extra layer of clothing was usually worn and the warmth from the fire was welcomed. We were delighted when a Christmas card arrived from Sue, Arthur and Tommy who had emigrated to Melbourne after Arthur had served his time in the army; they were all well and enjoying life in Australia. We weren't to know then that some 40 years later when visiting Carmine's sister near Melbourne that we would meet up with Sue and Tommy again; unfortunately Arthur had passed away but Sue and Stan her new husband were well and we had a lovely time with them including Tommy and his partner. As I say that was four decades away from now.

Andrew was now five and a half years old and like all the children in the village was excited as Christmas morning approached. The School and the sergeant's mess had parties with presents being given out by Santa Clause to all the children and although it didn't snow (not sure if it has ever snowed in Hong Kong), carols were sung at school and there was a lovely Christmas atmosphere in the village. Social evenings with entertainments, fancy dress dances and buffets were organised by various committees whilst lights and decorations were appearing in the NAFFI, school, library, and regimental messes adding to the happy feeling of Christmas. It was also a time when our thoughts were with our families at home, across the other side of the world and although we missed them, we would rather be here in Hong Kong.

Our friends and ourselves realised that it would be our last festive season together as army postings in1968 would inevitably take us to different spheres around the world and we all decided to have a memorable and enjoyable time with the children when we were invited to each other's homes for the usual drinks, food and fun.

We would always remember how the 'look see' lady, the fruit and veg. man and the other traders walked up and down the village hill carrying their wares. This was quite amazing but how the coolie carrying his baskets of coal on his bamboo pole stretched across his shoulders managed to shuffle up and down it was a feat that many a weight lifting athlete could not have competed with. Carmine decided to have some made-to-measure skirts and dresses to take home whilst I was measured for some long sleeved shirts from the tailor who had come from the nearby town of Yuen Long at prices so cheap that nobody back home would believe.

I spent the next few weeks going around the regiments, discussing physical training programmes with the battalion Training Officers and ensuring that the Assistant Physical Training Instructors were carrying out their roles in ensuring the fitness of their companies as I had discussed with them. It was extremely important that the swimming instruction for non-swimmers was continued and when I looked at the results of the tests that I had set, I could see that the percentage pass marks had gone up. I thanked all who were responsible for that success and informed the Commanding Officers through the 2ic.s accordingly. Although the coaching of teams participating in a variety of popular sports such as football, volleyball, rugby, athletics and cross country running was important, the encouragement of trying out new sports and recreational activities such as swimming, water polo, sub aqua and snorkelling, judo, tennis, orienteering, canoeing and sailing to name but a few was supported in general by Commanding Officers.

29 Mule Pack Company (Chinese Hong Kong soldiers) was always a joy to visit and when not mucking out the stables or exercising in the hills, they would be playing football or volleyball and they believed that they were fit to carry out their role for war with the amount of time that they spent hill walking. They were a cheery crowd and always made me welcome; they assured me that they could all swim and I had certainly played against some of them in the water polo league.

A letter arrived one morning from Ken. He had joined the Mounties. I smiled to myself and wished him good luck in my thoughts.

One afternoon the Brigadier sent for me. 'Please sit down Staff,' he said gesturing to the large arm chair adjacent to his desk.

'I've been tied up with meetings recently and haven't seen you for a couple of weeks but I hear that you and QMSI Goodwin have been working hard with the regiments and squadrons within the Brigade and I wish to say 'thank you.' The Commanding Officers are reporting that they will be sorry to see you go and admire your learning of the Gurkhali, the way you responded on active service in Borneo and the way that you do get the best out of the Gurkha soldier. I wish to say to you personally 'well done.' I know that you have a young son at the village school and I hear nothing but praise for Mrs. Gee for the work, help and support that she gives to groups around the village. Please tell her from me that it is appreciated by many people who no doubt will be seeing her shortly and telling her themselves.

'Thank-you sir, I am enjoying my posting to 48 brigade very much and I will pass your kind comments on to my wife.'

'However,' said the Brigadier, 'it will shortly be time for you to be posted and gain experience for the future which I believe if you continue in this vein will lead to further promotions. However I mustn't keep you in suspense any longer; your next posting is to the 1st Battalion (The Royal Highland Regiment) The Black Watch in Edinburgh which I believe is your home town. How do you feel about that?' he asked.

He must have seen my eyes light up and the smile on my face.

'I thought so,' he said. 'Congratulations' and he rose to shake my hand. 'I think that you should get off home and tell Mrs Gee, the good news. It looks like sometime about March or April but it will of course be confirmed within the next few days. Well done staff,' he said as I left his office in a daze.

On Saturday, we set off early to spend the day in Kowloon with the aim of either buying or earmarking items that we wanted to take home with us and we went into an electrical type shop that sold everything from the most up to date cameras with the latest photographic technology, much of it from Japan, record players, tape recorders and stereo equipment. We purchased a tape recorder that we liked and a Fujica Drive camera which would allow us to take photographs and have them made into slides; needless to say we had some photographs changed into slides by the shop and we bought a slide projector and a Polaroid instamatic camera which could take a photograph and be developed for us to view in about 15 seconds which allowed another photograph to be taken if the first one hadn't turned out quite right.

The following weekend we came down again to the large market off Nathan Road where some stall holders kept choices of records that could be copied on to blank recording tapes which could be played on our tape recorders. The cost including the tapes was very little and all our friends and most of the village frequented the market.

Carmine was now shopping for clothing of every kind to take home with us, not to mention, peril rings and other items of jewellery, some as gifts for the family; all which had an accompanied bona fide certificate for Customs. Although there was a weight limit some heavier clothing could be put in with our MFO boxes which would be returning by sea. There were also varieties of children's clothing to be purchased at very tempting prices and as Carmine kept saying, we were going to feel the cold when we got off that plane back home.

Instead of driving back home, we decided to park the car and catch the Star Ferry over to the Island, have lunch before tackling the stalls and the shops there. Andrew always enjoyed the excitement of the ferry trip with all the Chinese junks and boats sometimes almost bumping into the ferries. As always the hustle and bustle on the streets could only be matched by life in Kowloon but I felt that although we were looking forward to going home, we would miss this world of bustling people; noise from traffic and Mah-jong games, stalls selling all sorts of commodities including toys and trinkets. Aromas of food emanating from sizzling cooking pots and pans on fired up grills, curled around every street corner enticing customers to sample.

We decided to have a Chinese meal and when it started raining, we quickly decided on a restaurant that looked clean at least from the outside. One was not always sure until one had entered and had a quick look around inside especially at the toilets. The menu had a good choice of Cantonese food which originated from Canton, a town just over the Chinese border whereas Mandarin cuisine came from the more northerly regions of China. As always, we decided to choose a meal each and share between the three of us with an extra rice dish and a starter of spring rolls with soft drinks. We said 'yes,' when asked if we used chop sticks, with the help of a spoon for Andrew. We had a most enjoyable meal for around fifteen HK dollars [approx £8). When we came out of the restaurant, it had stopped raining and the sun was once again shining on Hong Kong. We strolled through the streets enjoying the atmosphere, browsing the shops but always ensuring that one of us took Andrew's hand. By this time, we were quite laden with shopping and Andrew was beginning to get tired. We decided to head back across the harbour, buy an ice cream at the YMCA en route to the car and head through Kowloon and up the TWISK to home. As usual Andrew was sound asleep before we reached the end of Nathan Road

We had now to start thinking about our furniture and household goods that would be sent home through the army system under the Quartermaster's Department. Large MFO boxes were issued and we already had the made to measure chests for our hand carved furniture; we were now able to start packing.

The mess had held a Saint Valentine's Fancy Dress buffet and dance which was good fun and enjoyed by all. We were certainly going to miss Ah Moi when we got home for the many chores including babysitting that she carried out. We thought about smuggling her home in an MFO box but realised that we just had to say good bye

Andrew had settled into school so well and had lots of friends. We knew that he would miss them but like all children of army parents, he would adjust and retain his good experiences and make new friends at his next school. He would no doubt like the rest of us miss the warm weather, swimming in the outdoor pools, barbecues in the garden, playing out of doors on most days and being spoilt by our Amah.

John Smart, a sergeant from 18 Light Regt popped round to ask if he could have first refusal on the car which was the normal system when someone was leaving the Colony.

It was early March when we again rolled off the ferry and drove around Hong Kong Island, realising that it would be our last visit to the Island. We drove to Stanley Market, bought some bits and pieces, walked along the beach with a fresh breeze blowing in our faces and ran up the beach swinging Andrew as he held on to our hands. Crossing back on the ferry, we looked out to sea and knew that we would never forget our Hong Kong experience. We gave Andrew a special hug and I think we had a tear in our eyes but maybe it was just the breeze.

The weeks rolled by so quickly and Mick and Irene and all our friends gave us a wonderful send off and we all promised to try to keep in touch. The Brigadier, staff officers and officers of the Gurkha Regiments shook my hand, thanked me for my work and all wished me well for the future. I was sorry to be leaving friends from the mess but that was army life and we all had to move on. I know Carmine felt sad leaving her friends in the village and we both said a special good bye to Ah Moi who gave Andrew a cuddle with tears in her eyes.

On the 30th March, the coach rolled up the hill of Sek Kong village bound for Kai Tak Airport with all the families that were going home to UK. Life in the forces was a constant flow of people, their families and their luggage going around the world and coming back. It had taken us 38 hours to journey to Hong Kong but homeward bound, our flight on an RAF VC10, stopping over to refuel on the island of Guam and again on Cyprus, took only fourteen hours flying time. We touched down at RAF Lynham in Wiltshire, joined the waiting coach which took us to Kings Cross Station in

London where we boarded the train for the final stage of our journey to Edinburgh, our home.